THE VICTORIOUS, OVERCOMING LIFE

(A Verse-by-Verse Study of the Book of Colossians)

THE VICTORIOUS, OVERCOMING LIFE

(A Verse-by-Verse Study of the Book of Colossians)

By
Frederick K.C. Price, Ph.D.

Crenshaw Christian Center Publishers
Los Angeles, California

Unless otherwise indicated, all Scripture quotations are taken from the *King James Version* of the Bible.

The Victorious, Overcoming Life
(A Verse-by-Verse Study of the Book of Colossians)
ISBN 1-883798-00-0
Copyright © 1993 by
Frederick K.C. Price
P.O. Box 90000
Los Angeles, CA 90009

Published by Crenshaw Christian Center Publishers
7901 South Vermont Avenue
Los Angeles, California 90044

Contents

Introduction

The Epistle to the Colossians was written by Paul to the church at Colossae during his first imprisonment in Rome (around 60 AD). Colossae was about 100 miles east of Ephesus. Tradition tells us that the church probably was established by Epaphras (Col. 1:7), who was a convert of Paul's during his three-year ministry in Ephesus.

The people of Colossae apparently enjoyed some degree of sophistication. This was evidenced by their readiness to accept ideas developed from the complex mixture of Greek philosophy and pagan religions that later became known as *gnosticism*, an heretical belief. This belief is still found in some cults today.

Gnosticism stressed salvation through "intuitive" knowledge rather than through the new birth, and it assigned to Jesus a place subordinate to the Godhead or Trinity. Also, this doctrine replaced the redemptive work of Christ on Calvary with an emphasis on personal works and fostered the worship of angelic beings.

The Apostle Paul responded to this erroneous doctrine by describing the full authority assigned to Christ and showing man's complete redemption in and through Him. He encouraged the Colossians to learn to walk in the grace and liberty provided by Jesus on the cross, and he taught against religious bondage of any sort.

This book is not meant to be a scholarly study, but rather a practical contemporary commentary on Paul's letter. I want to share with you the benefits of applying the principles and concepts found in this letter to your every-day life.

We are living 1,900 years later, yet Holy Spirit-inspired truths are timeless. The information found in this epistle will help you to achieve — and to live to the fullest — the victorious, overcoming life in Christ.

One of the beautiful things about ministering from the New Covenant (New Testament) books is that, as you go through them verse by verse and chapter by chapter, you encounter every facet of today's problems. That excites and thrills me.

What I am teaching from the Book of Colossians is not by any means all there is to teach from this important epistle! However, these comments are what the Holy Spirit revealed to me concerning this letter and its application to our daily lives. I trust this book will be a blessing to you.

Frederick K.C. Price, Ph.D.
Pastor, Crenshaw Christian Center
Los Angeles, California

1

Walking Worthy of the Lord
(Col. 1:1-13)

Paul, an apostle of Jesus Christ by the will of God, and Timotheus our brother, To the saints and faithful brethren in Christ which are at Colosse: Grace be unto you, and peace, from God our Father and the Lord Jesus Christ. We give thanks to God and the Father of our Lord Jesus Christ, praying always for you, Since we heard of your faith in Christ Jesus, and of the love which ye have to all the saints. For the hope which is laid up for you in heaven, whereof ye heard before in the word of the truth of the gospel; Which is come unto you, as it is in all the world; and bringeth forth fruit, as it doth also in you, since the day ye heard of it, and knew the grace of God in truth: As ye also learned of Epaphras our dear fellowservant, who is for you a faithful minister of Christ; Who also declared unto us your love in the Spirit.

(Col. 1:1-8)

The above verses, into which this letter was organized by the translators of the King James Version, actually are one long salutation, or greeting, from Paul to the members of the congregation that met at Colossae.

Paul had not founded this church, nor had he ever visited it, as far as we can tell. But the man named Epaphras, who was their *"faithful minister of Christ"*

1

(v.7), had been one of Paul's converts in Ephesus. Therefore, Paul felt a responsibility for the Colossian church that went beyond what he may have felt for churches founded by other apostles or their disciples.

Colossae was located in Asia Minor, in what is today the southwestern part of Turkey. About 600 years before Christ, it had been a great city during the days of Persia. However, Rome moved the trade route north to Pergamum which caused the growth of Laodicea and the decline of Colossae.

In spite of Colossae's declining importance, the Colossians were exposed to the pagan ideas and philosophy of Greece and Rome. At any rate, Paul apparently had heard about some of the beliefs that were beginning to be entertained by some of the Christians in Colossae, and these errors concerned him.

He was especially concerned about this because, when he first heard of the assembly of believers at Colossae, he had been impressed with their love in the Spirit (v.8).

After Paul greeted the church, he told them of the things that he was praying about for them. Verses 9 and 10 form a prayer that any pastor can pray over his flock. This is the prayer that I pray over *my* congregation.

> For this cause we also, since the day we heard it, do not cease to pray for you, and to desire that ye might be filled with the knowledge of his will in all wisdom and spiritual understanding; That ye might walk worthy of the Lord unto all pleasing, being fruitful in every good work, and increasing in the knowledge of God.
>
> **(Col. 1:9,10)**

My desire for the people at Crenshaw Christian Center is that they might be filled with the knowledge of God's will in all wisdom and spiritual understanding. That also is my desire for *you*.

The keynote of *my* own life is to walk worthy of the Lord unto all pleasing (Col. 1:10). As born-again people, new creatures in Christ Jesus (see 2 Cor. 5:17), we have been given the privilege of becoming the sons of God. I do not believe many of us realize what a privilege that is!

God was God before He ever thought of creating us. God was God before He ever created the world. He does not need us in order to be God. He *was* God; He *is* God; and He always *will be* God, whether mankind exists or not.

Therefore, it is a privilege beyond imagining that God has granted us through Jesus Christ to become His children and to be part of His family. Too many of us take this for granted. We forget it is a privilege to call God ''Father.''

Do you realize that angels, who are mighty in power, mighty in strength and mighty in wisdom and knowledge, cannot call God ''Father''? But here is *man*, a puny speck of dust, a molecule on the sea of eternity; and yet, those of us who *choose* Jesus have the right to call Almighty God our heavenly Father.

Are you worthy to call Him that? Of course we are not worthy *in ourselves*, but we can live worthy of that privilege *in* Christ Jesus. *Walking worthy of the Lord* means living in such a way that the privilege granted to you of being a child of God is being exhibited to the

3

world. Your life-style shows whether you are living worthy of the honor bestowed upon you or not.

Instead of living like the devil, we need to begin living like children of God.

Bring Forth Fruit, Increase in Knowledge

Walking worthily includes being fruitful in good works and increasing in knowledge, in addition to living a righteous, Christ-like life-style. But the fruits are a result of our relationship with God, not the cause of it. We cannot use "fruits" to *earn* a place as God's children.

Are you bringing forth fruit? That is the "name of the game"; that is why a tree is planted — to bring forth fruit. Jesus told a parable about a man who went into his vineyard and found a fig tree that had no fruit on it (Luke 13:6-9).

The man said to his gardener, "I have looked for figs on this tree for three years, and I have never found any. Cut this tree down. Why are you leaving it here, taking up room?"

But the gardener said, "Sir, leave it another year. Let me fertilize it, dig around it, weed it, water it and take care of it. Give it another year, Lord. If it does not show any fruit by that time, we will cut it down."

Are you bringing forth fruit? Have you brought forth any fruit? Or, are you like that tree, taking up space, soaking up nutrients and not giving anything back? Are you a liability, or are you an asset to the Kingdom of God? Are you a help in your local church or a hindrance and an obstacle?

You may say you are a Christian, but Jesus said the tree is known by its fruit. Citrus trees — lemons, oranges, grapefruits, tangerines — all look very much alike. The leaves look the same, the coloring is the same and the shape of the trees is the same. The average person cannot tell exactly what kind of tree it is *until they see the fruit.*

Can people tell by looking at your life what kind of tree you are? Also, do you realize that you can increase, not only in fruitfulness, but in the knowledge of God?

Many Christians are just as they were five years ago or when they first got saved. They are not increasing! In order to increase, you must apply the Word in your life. To increase, you must read the Word each time in a fresh light, as if you had never read it before. That way, you will always find insight and knowledge that you did not have. If you do not expect to find anything new in the Word, you will not find it.

Partakers of the Inheritance

> **Strengthened with all might, according to his glorious power, unto all patience and longsuffering with joyfulness; Giving thanks unto the Father, which hath made us meet to be partakers of the inheritance of the saints in light.**
>
> **(Col. 1:11,12, emphasis mine)**

In the twelfth verse, the word *meet* used by the translators of the King James Version can be a little misleading. The Greek word there actually means

5

"able."[1] Paul was saying you need always to give thanks to God who made you *able* to be partakers of the inheritance of the saints.

Just because you are able to do something does not mean you are *going* to do it. Many Christians have talents and abilities, but they are not allowing God to have the use of them. Perhaps you are *able* to do something, but you are letting others assume the responsibility instead of you.

If God wants you to do something specifically, He will let you know. If He does not let you know, simply wait until He does. But at least make your talents and abilities available to Him.

Notice that Paul said the Father *made* us able to be partakers. *US* means everyone. I like that about God. He puts things on such a level that anyone can partake of the inheritance to the degree he or she chooses. No one has "a corner on the market." No one has any more of an advantage than anyone else.

What *is* the inheritance of the saints in light (v. 12)?

An inheritance is something that is left to a person or persons by someone who has passed on to the next life. Usually, an inheritance is named or listed in a last will and testament. Before anyone dies, if that person is wise, his or her assets are listed in a legal document with instructions as to what is to be done with them.

Those assets are called an inheritance to the people who are to receive them. The title of the collected books

---

[1]James Strong, *THE EXHAUSTIVE CONCORDANCE OF THE BIBLE* (Nashville: Abingdon, Greek Dictionary, p. 37, #2427).

of the Bible written since the time of Jesus is called the New Testament, which really means the ''New Will,'' ''New Covenant'' or ''New Agreement.''

A new will supersedes an old one. When it comes time for a will to be filed and fulfilled, the court does not go back to an old one. The last authorized will to be made before the person's death is the one that is considered legal.

If someone leaves you a million dollars in one will, then later makes a new one and leaves you $10,000,000, which one would you take? That is how much difference exists between the Old Covenant and the New Covenant. Paul tells us in Hebrews 8:6 that believers in Christ have a ''better covenant.''

Jesus did something no one else has ever done. He made a ''will,'' then He died. *But* He came back to life in order to be the executor of the will and to see to it that no one could cheat His heirs out of what belonged to them. He made it possible for us to have it all.

However, just as with an earthly will, you have to let those in charge know that you are one of the heirs. You have to *appropriate* what is yours.

Every year, hundreds of thousands of dollars go to state governments because people do not cash in on their inheritances. There are millions of dollars held by banks in every state because people are entitled to money that was left to them, but they never claimed it.

Delivered From the Power of Darkness

Who *hath* delivered us from the power of

7

darkness, and *hath* translated us into the kingdom of his dear Son.

(Col. 1:13, italics mine)

In verse 13, notice the word *hath*. That is an old English word that corresponds to our present-day word *has*. God *has* delivered us from the power of darkness. That lets us know that deliverance is not future tense. Deliverance already has come.

Therefore, every born-again person has been delivered: *I* am delivered; *you* are delivered; *we* are delivered. We *ARE* (present tense) set free, because God *has already* (past tense) set us at liberty from the power of darkness.

If we have been delivered, we must have been in some kind of bondage. We must have been in a place from which we needed to be delivered. And if you have been delivered *from* somewhere, you must be delivered *to* somewhere else.

It is important to understand where you have been delivered from in order to appreciate where you have been delivered to.

The word translated *power* in verse 13 is the Greek word *exousia*, which literally means "authority."[2] A better translation would be: "Who hath delivered us from the *authority* of darkness."

Using "power" as it is translated there gives the wrong impression. Satan and his troops obviously still have some power — not the power he had in heaven — but still some supernatural power. However, the

---

[2]Ibid, p. 30, #1849.

authority of the least Christian can override Satan's power and put him on the run.

The Word says that the enemy has power. But Jesus defeated him. Therefore, *we* have the authority over *all* the power of the enemy. Jesus said:

> **Behold, I give unto you *power* to tread on serpents and scorpions, and over all the *power* of the enemy: and nothing shall by any means hurt you.**
> **(Luke 10:19, italics mine)**

The first *power* in the above verse also is the Greek word *exousia,* which basically means ''authority.''[3] But the second time *power* is used in the King James version — *over all the power of the enemy* — the Greek word is *dunamis,* which means ''ability.''[4] So in Luke 10:19, Jesus was saying:

> **I give you all My *authority* to tread on serpents and scorpions, and over all of the *ability* that the enemy still possesses. And don't worry, nothing can hurt you as long as you use the *authority* of My name.**

That means Satan has no more *authority* over us. He no longer has any *legal right* to lord it over us. However, we do need to remember that he does not play fair. He is the father of all crookedness, the father of lies (John 8:44). He is a cheat and a usurper. If you give him an inch, he will take twenty-five miles. If you blink your eye at what he is doing, he will try to take your head off!

---

[3]Ibid., p. 30, *1849.*
[4]Ibid., p. 24, *1411.*

Delivered Into the Kingdom of Jesus Christ

> . . . and *hath* translated us into the kingdom of
> his dear Son.
>
> **(Col. 1:13, italics mine)**

In the last part of verse 13, there is that word *hath*
again. That means we already *have been* translated into
the Kingdom of Jesus. *Darkness* in the Bible always is
used as a contradiction, or an absolute opposite to *light*.

The Word says that God is light (Isa. 60:20, Mic.
7:8), and when Jesus was on earth, He said that He
is light (John 8:12). In spiritual things, Satan and
demons are referred to as *darkness*.

In the Bible, any time there is a reference to *light*
or to *darkness*, the Holy Spirit is talking about spiritual
things. The only exception is when a literal *day* or *night*
is involved. Otherwise, the terms are used figuratively
to illustrate spiritual truths.

Unfortunately, most churches have not been
informed that Christians already have been delivered.
Satan is still illegally lording it over many Christians
because of their lack of knowledge (Hos. 4:6). When
you were born again, you entered into the Kingdom
of God's dear Son. Jesus said in John's gospel:

> . . . Verily, verily, I say unto thee, Except a man
> be born again, he cannot see [come to know] the
> *kingdom of God*. . . . Verily, verily [truly, or "I am
> telling you the truth"], I say unto thee, Except a man
> be born of water and of the Spirit, he cannot enter
> into the kingdom of God.
>
> **(John 3:3,5, italics mine)**

You are not waiting for Jesus to come back to get into the Kingdom. *All* Christians are in the Kingdom of God's dear Son *right now* by virtue of the new birth. *Jesus is our King. He is our Lord right now!*

It is true that there is still a kingdom coming that is referred to in the Gospel of Matthew as "*the kingdom of heaven,*" which will be a *political system* that will operate in this earth realm. It will be a theocracy; "*theos*" means "God." It will be a kingdom that will be presided over by God and Christ. And it will be a political system that God himself will set up — *that kingdom is coming,* but we are in the Kingdom of God's dear Son right now. This is a spiritual kingdom which encompasses God's reign and rule throughout the universe — and we are in that Kingdom! How did we get into it? *By being translated into it at the new birth.* We left the kingdom of darkness, and we are in Jesus' Kingdom — that means that all the benefits of the Kingdom belong to us, the citizens of the Kingdom.

This book that we call the "New Covenant," the "New Contract," the "New Testament" or the "New Will," spells out for us our legal rights. In fact, the New Testament could be referred to as our "*BILL OF RIGHTS,*" or literally, "*BILL OF RIGHTEOUSNESS.*" It means the bill concerning our right-standing with God, and it spells out for us all that belongs to us as citizens of the Kingdom.

> **Who hath delivered us from the power of darkness, and hath translated us into the kingdom of his dear Son.**
>
> **(Col. 1:13)**

11

If God has translated us into the Kingdom of His dear Son, that presupposes that the *Kingdom of His dear Son* must be in existence right now. For if it were not, how could we be translated into it?

Hath translated us, ''not is translating'' us, not ''going to translate'' us — but *''hath''* — *it is already done!* If I am in the *Kingdom of His dear Son,* that means *His dear Son,* not the kingdom of darkness, has lordship and rulership over me.

I want to share a revelation with you concerning the Kingdom of God's dear Son. When I first received Christ as my Savior, somehow I knew that I should make prayer a part of my life. I remember having heard a prayer which went something like this: *''Our Father, which art in heaven, hallowed be thy name,''* etc. In fact, someone put music to this prayer and made a very beautiful song out of it. We commonly call this prayer, ''The Lord's Prayer.''

I joined a particular denomination that had a worship liturgy, which simply means a mode of worship. Every Sunday we did the same thing. All the congregational singing was done from a hymnal or song book, and in the front part of the book was the format we would use in the worship service.

One of the things we did as part of this worship liturgy was to quote what is called, ''The Lord's Prayer.''

In my own private prayer time, I thought I was supposed to start out by praying this prayer every time and ending with, ''And now, heavenly Father, bless my mother, bless my father, bless my wife and my children, bless this person and that person, bless this

and bless that, and give me this and give me that, and
fix this and fix that, do this and do that, etc., etc., in
Jesus' Name. Amen.''

I thought that was prayer. Every prayer I prayed
started out with, *''Our Father, which art in heaven.''* In
fact, I thought I was not praying if I did not start out
with ''The Lord's Prayer.''

I want to be very clear about what I am about to
say. I am not going to tell *you* what to do or what not
to do. My name is not God. I want you to understand
that. If you cannot receive it, *it is not for you.* The Bible
says that he who has ears to hear, let him hear. If you
cannot receive this, don't get upset but just take what
you can, and what you cannot receive, leave alone.

I believe the Lord showed this to me, and it has
personally helped me in my own prayer life.

I am not shooting down anyone's method of
worship, but I want to point something out to you,
so that as you go into your worship time alone or with
a group or with your denomination, or wherever, you
will at least be more aware of what you are saying. If
you believe that what you are saying is right, then
continue on with it. But if not, then you need to get
off the wrong train and onto the one you believe is the
right one.

In Matthew, chapter 6, beginning with verse 9,
Jesus says:

> **After this manner therefore pray ye: Our Father
> which art in heaven, Hallowed be thy name. Thy
> kingdom come. Thy will be done in earth, as it is in
> heaven. Give us this day our daily bread. And forgive
> us our debts, as we forgive our debtors. And lead us**

**not into temptation, but deliver us from evil: For thine
is the kingdom, and the power, and the glory, for
ever. Amen.**

Notice the words ''THY KINGDOM COME.''
Remember Colossians 1:13, which states, ''WHO
HATH DELIVERED US FROM THE POWER OF
DARKNESS, AND HATH TRANSLATED US INTO
THE KINGDOM....''

To say, ''THY KINGDOM COME,'' is to say the
kingdom has not yet come. Because if the Kingdom
had already come, you would not say, ''THY
KINGDOM COME,'' you would say, ''THY KING-
DOM IS HERE,'' or something like that.

When Jesus uttered these words, He had not yet
gone to Calvary, nor had He defeated Satan, nor had
He risen from the dead, nor had He ascended to the
Father, and the New Covenant had not yet come into
being. When Jesus uttered these words, He was still
in the last days of the *Old Covenant.*

Many people get confused when they read
Matthew, Mark, Luke and John because,
unfortunately, these books are labeled as being part
of the New Testament. Actually, Matthew, Mark, Luke
and John ought to be the last four books of the Old
Testament and the Book of Acts should be the first
book of the New Testament. The New Testament could
not come into being until after Jesus' resurrection and
ascension to the right hand of the Father. Everything
He said and everything He did before He *died, rose* and
ascended was done under the Old Covenant. He
ministered in the very last days of the Old Testament.

Jesus never told us to pray this prayer. He said, "AFTER THIS MANNER." He did not say, "Repeat after me." The reason Jesus prayed, "Thy Kingdom come," was because the Kingdom could not come until He went back to the Father. That was the only way they could pray at that point.

Now we are on the other side of Calvary. We are on the other side of the Resurrection. We are on the other side of the Ascension; therefore, we do not say, "THY KINGDOM COME" — *HIS KINGDOM HAS ALREADY COME!* We are in the Kingdom right now. We have been translated into the Kingdom of His Dear Son! To deny that the Kingdom has come is to deny Calvary, the Resurrection and the fact that Jesus has ascended to the Father.

Paul has told us that God has delivered us from the power of darkness and has translated us into the Kingdom. God could not translate us into the Kingdom, unless the Kingdom was here to be translated into.

Notice Matthew 9:13, which states, "AND LEAD US NOT INTO TEMPTATION, BUT DELIVER US FROM EVIL." The word "evil" in this verse should literally be rendered, "THE EVIL ONE." You cannot be delivered from evil without being delivered from the "evil one." Evil exists because of the evil one. When you get rid of the skin cancer, you will not have any sores on your body. If you get rid of leprosy, your flesh will be clean. If you get rid of the cause, you will not have the symptoms. Evil is symptomatic of the evil one; if you get rid of the evil one, you will have no more symptoms of evil. Satan is the evil one, and darkness is a characteristic of his kingdom.

15

ce Colossians tells us we have been delivered from the kingdom of darkness (evil), how can we still pray, "Deliver us from evil?" Jesus has died, gone to hell (Hades), served our sentence, rose from the dead — He has defeated death, hell and the grave, ascended into heaven, sat down at the right hand of God and is now in the process of making His enemies His footstool.

He has given us the authority to use His Name. He has given us the Word of the living God. He has given us the Holy Spirit, and He has given us the commission to go and preach the Gospel to all the world. He said these signs shall follow them that believe: In My name they shall lay hands on the sick and the sick shall recover. Jesus said and did all these things — how can anyone say that God's Kingdom has not yet come? THE KINGDOM IS ALREADY HERE, AND WE HAVE *ALREADY* BEEN DELIVERED FROM THE EVIL ONE! However, you have to know that and you have to act on that in order for it to do you any personal good.

The passage in Romans 10:17, says: "SO THEN FAITH COMETH BY HEARING." Think about it, if every week you pray "THE OUR FATHER," you hear it with your ears, you even say it with your mouth. You are not only hearing what the preacher or the priest is saying, you are hearing it out of your own mouth as you repeat it, audibly in unison, with the rest of the people. You are saying, "THY KINGDOM COME" — you heard that, and so faith for that came. You are still thinking the Kingdom is coming. You have great faith for the Kingdom to come, but you do not have faith that the Kingdom is here, because you are not hearing what you ought to hear.

If you continue to hear, "DELIVER US FROM THE EVIL ONE," and every time you hear it, faith for that comes, that will be as high as your faith will be able to go. Your faith cannot go any higher than the Word you receive. If the Word you receive is oriented toward the Old Covenant, then your faith is going to operate in Old-Covenant orientation and not in the New Covenant.

When you start hearing that God has already delivered you from the power of darkness and translated you into the Kingdom of His dear Son, then you will rise into the rarefied atmosphere of God's very best, and begin to operate in the benefits of the New Covenant. The devil will no longer be able to lord it over you. He will buzz around like some dumb fly, but you can pick up the can of "Raid," the Word of God, and spray that pest — zap! And you will knock him out!

I am not telling you how to pray. I have merely presented what I believe the Bible is saying. You can take it or leave it. If you want to keep on praying for God to deliver you, it is all right with me. But thank God, I know I am delivered. My heavenly Father told me that He delivered me. The Bible says it is impossible for God to lie, so if He told me I am delivered, I MUST BE DELIVERED!

Some Christians might say, "Yes, well I don't feel very delivered." That is the problem, they are going by how they feel instead of by the Word of the eternal God. It makes no difference how you feel about it. You are not delivered from one kingdom into another *because you feel like it.* You are delivered because God said so. The moment you begin to believe that, confess it, and act on it, then you will feel delivered. But you cannot feel it first, then get it.

You are delivered because God said you were! Begin to confess that with your mouth, and faith will come. Then you will be able to rise up and live in the blessings of the Kingdom in which you have been placed.

Many Christians run around begging, whining, crying and talking about the cost of living, and so forth. They confess they can hardly make it and do not know what to do. If every born-again person would believe that God made this earth, and that He can and does provide for His children, what a different impact we would make on the world!

Do you realize that God *knows* how long we are going to be here? He knows we will be provided for until the glorious day of the Resurrection.

2
Jesus, Lord of All
(Col. 1:14-20)

The Psalmist said:

Let the redeemed of the Lord say so, whom he hath redeemed from the hand of the enemy.
(Ps. 107:2)

According to the New Testament, we *are* the redeemed of the Lord already:

In whom we have redemption through his blood, even the forgiveness of sins.
(Col. 1:14)

We are not *trying* to get redeemed. We are not *going to be* redeemed in the future, somewhere in the sweet bye-and-bye, over there on the other side. That word *hath* shows up again in this verse, and it means our redemption *has already* (past tense) been accomplished.

If you have accepted Christ as your Savior and Lord, you are redeemed. If you are redeemed, that means you have been bought back out of the prison house of Satan. That means you are a free person.

19

However, *redemption* affects us in three different areas: spirit, soul and body.

You might say the price of redeeming man from Satan was paid once and for all, but man receives the restoration from bondage in stages: past, present and future.

As far as God is concerned, your spirit, soul and body *are* already redeemed.

As far as your appropriation of redemption is concerned, only your spirit — the real you who lives inside your body — has received the fullness of redemption and become a new creature (2 Cor. 5:17).

In terms of earthly time, however, your soul is being redeemed from day to day, as you bring your mind into conformity to the image of Jesus (Rom. 8:29). And your body will receive the fullness of its redemption at the Resurrection (Phil. 3:21).

When you are born again, the only thing about you that is immediately affected, immediately changed, is the real you, the spirit.

In order to understand this, we need to look at what the Apostle Paul wrote to the church at Rome.

> **I beseech you therefore, brethren, by the mercies of God, that ye present your bodies a living sacrifice, holy, acceptable unto God, which is your reasonable service. And be not conformed to this world: but be ye transformed by the renewing of your mind.**
> **(Rom. 12:1,2)**

First, Paul is saying to *present* your bodies as a *living* sacrifice. And the sense of *to present* here is the same as that used in *presenting* the animal sacrifices unto God. The difference is that animal sacrifices were dead, and we are to offer on the altar our bodies while life is yet in us, while we are yet in the world.

What Are Living Sacrifices?

You can personalize this verse by saying, "God is beseeching me, by His mercies, to present *my* body as a living sacrifice. If *"my"* possesses a body, then *"my"* and *body* must be separate. If Paul was talking about body, soul and spirit all being one inseparable unit, he would have said, "Present yourself."

When Paul tells us to present our bodies and renew our minds, he is talking to the spirit-part of us on the inside which is created in the image of the Father. Until Jesus returns, and we move into the fullness of the redemption process, the obligation to do something about our bodies and our souls is on *us*.

The glorious news is that if God tells us through the Apostle Paul to do this, then obviously, it is possible for us to do it. And it is possible because Jesus *showed* us how to live through His life, the Holy Spirit *told* us how to live by inspiring the writings of the Word, and the Godhead *lives* within us.

The *works of Satan* which Jesus came to earth to destroy (1 John 3:8) has affected all men, the earth and all parts of mankind. Redemption began the process of the restoration of all things. Praise the Lord, the salvation of the spirit (the real us) came first, because that sets us into the Kingdom of God. Redemption of the spirit causes us to have eternal life, because the life of God became an eternal part of us.

We *gave* ourselves to Christ when we were born again. Then Paul said that we need to give our bodies and our souls to Him as well. That is a progressive experience.

> **Wherefore, my beloved, as ye have always obeyed, not as in my presence only, but now much more in my absence, work out [complete] your own salvation with fear and trembling.**
>
> **(Phil. 2:12)**

Obviously, Paul cannot mean that we are *to earn* our born-again experience, for that would contradict all of the things told us by the Holy Spirit about Christ's work accomplished on the cross. Therefore, Paul has to be talking about the "working out" of the renewing of our minds and the bringing of our bodies under authority.

You, the real you, belongs to God, but your body and your soul belong to you and have to be changed into the likeness of Jesus by *your* choices and through the power of the Holy Spirit.

There is another point I would like to make concerning the soul which is found in the book of James. The author called the people to whom his letter was written *my brethren* (James 1:2). You do not call someone *brethren* unless you are in the same family.

James was writing to believers in Christ who formerly had believed in Judaism. They were still Israelites by earthly race, but no longer Jews by religion. Now they were called Christians and were members of a heavenly race.

James 5:14 verifies that James was writing to the Church, and not to his brothers still in Judaism.

> **Is any sick among you? Let him call for the elders of the church . . . .**
>
> **(James 5:14)**

So it is established that James is writing to the Church. In fact, none of the letters (epistles) were written to sinners or to secularists. All of them were written to believers, members of the family of God.

> **Wherefore lay apart all filthiness and superfluity of naughtiness, and receive with meekness the engrafted word, which is able to *save* your souls.**
>
> **(James 1:21, italics mine)**

You Cannot Earn Salvation

Some may say, "But I thought my soul was already saved!"

Why would James write this to the Body of Christ if their souls were saved already? If this were already done, he would have said: "Receive with teachableness the engrafted word which *has* saved your souls."

However, the saving of the soul is an ongoing process, a replacing of the old nature trained and programed by the world with the things of God. This must be done by studying and hearing the Word and through prayer.

The salvation of the spirit is instantaneous. You are born again instantly. Redemption of the real you is a free gift, and all you have to do is to receive it. But the soul and the physical body have to be brought up to the standard of Jesus as found in the Bible until such time as He returns or we go to be with Him.

Please do not misunderstand what I am saying! There may be some who will want to think I am saying that we are not born again and saved by the blood of Jesus. *I DID NOT SAY THAT!*

If you have been born again, in the sense of eternal salvation, you are as saved as you will ever be. The price has been paid by Jesus. God is satisfied. Divine justice is satisfied, and as far as God is concerned, your salvation is an accomplished fact. Jesus does not have to do anything else.

However, the manifestation of perfection has not yet come, although it has been bought and paid for. The real you on the inside of your body has become the custodian of your soul and body and it is accountable for conforming you to Jesus.

In simple terms, it is like someone going to the store and buying something for you. They give you the receipt, and you can prove that it belongs to you. But it has not been delivered yet. The manifestation has not yet come, but when it does, it is already paid for. You do not have to pay for it again.

Romans 8:19 clarifies this further:

> **For the earnest expectation of the creature waiteth for the manifestation of the sons of God.**

If the creatures are waiting for the *manifestation* of the sons of God, it is obvious that the sons of God have not yet been manifested. Otherwise, the creatures would not be waiting.

> **For the creature was made subject to vanity, not willingly, but by reason of him who hath subjected the same in hope, Because the creature itself shall be delivered from the bondage of corruption into the glorious liberty of the children of God. For we know that the whole creation groaneth and travaileth in pain together until now. And not only they, but ourselves also, which have the firstfruits of the Spirit, even we ourselves groan within ourselves, waiting for the adoption, to wit, the *redemption of our body.***
>
> **(Rom. 8:20-23, italics mine)**

Notice that Paul did not say in verse 23, *waiting for our adoption* but *waiting for the adoption . . .* of our body.

Again, he is talking about us (Christians) being new creatures who, together with the whole of creation, groan *within ourselves* (v. 23) for total redemption.

When the physical manifestation of your redemptive body comes, you will never get old. You will never have a wrinkle. You will never be sick again. No more arthritis, gray hair or bald heads! We will be eternally young and beautiful. *But this has not yet happened.*

I realize what I have just explained sounds different from the traditional religious explanation, but it *is* the Word of God.

New Creatures Have Old Flesh

You are born again; you have become a new creature in Christ Jesus and old things have passed away (2 Cor. 5:17) — but all of this happens in the spirit, not in the flesh. This should be obvious. If you have false teeth the day before you get saved, you will still have them the day after. Old things did not pass away in the body. You are the same flesh you were before salvation.

The "old things" that passed away are: alienation from God, spiritual death, condemnation and sin-consciousness. All of those things passed away, but the body remained as it was.

Thank God for the blood of Jesus through which we have redemption, even the forgiveness of our sins.

> Who is the *image* of the invisible God, the first-born of every creature.
> (Col. 1:15, italics mine)

What is an *image?* An image is a likeness, a replica. In this case, Paul was saying the original is invisible, but Jesus is an exact replica of the original Being who is God.

In First Timothy 3:16, Paul states this in a little different way:

> And without controversy great is the mystery of godliness: God was *manifest* [visible] in the flesh.
> (Italics mine)

The Bible tells us this is a mystery. A mystery in the Bible does not mean something God is secretly withholding from us. It simply means that whatever is a *mystery* is something that in our natural minds we cannot understand.

I would say that ninety-nine percent of what we operate on in the natural world we take by faith. Someone told us about George Washington, Christopher Columbus and Daniel Boone. *We* do not personally know these men or what they did. We were not even there when they were supposed to have lived. Yet, by natural faith, we take lock, stock and barrel what history books record about them. Bible faith should operate the same way that natural faith does.

God does not require us to understand everything He says or does. He just requires us to believe.

Your boss has agreed to pay you next week, but how do you know he has the money? You cannot check his bank account. You must believe *by faith* in the man's word that you will get paid.

You go out and buy a house, committing yourself to make thirty years worth of payments. How do you know that you are going to have the money? You are buying that house by faith. At least give God as much trust as you do your boss.

Let's look at First Timothy 3:16 in its entirety:

> **And without controversy great is the mystery of godliness: God was manifest in the flesh, justified in the Spirit, seen of angels, preached unto the Gentiles, believed on in the world, received up into glory.**

Who was Paul talking about? He was talking about Jesus, who was God manifested in the flesh. Jesus said it: *"He that hath seen me hath seen the Father"* (John 14:9). That is a mystery. I cannot understand it. I do not attempt to understand it. I just accept it and live in the victory of it.

Firstborn of Many Brethren

Back to Colossians 1:15:

Who is the image of the invisible God, the *firstborn* **of every creature. (italics mine)**

I am emphasizing this because I want to illustrate something by reasoning from the known to the unknown, the accepted principle of reasoning. You cannot reason from the *unknown*, so you begin with what is *known*.

Who is that verse speaking about? Paul is writing about Jesus. *"Firstborn"* implies second, third, fourth and fifth-born, and on and on. Also, the word implies that Jesus was the first of God's sons; yet, He already was God's Son.

What that verse says is that Jesus was *the first* of many. Paul was not talking about His virgin birth, because there is not going to be even one more born that way, much less *many*.

He could not be talking about physical births, because Jesus was not the first person to be born through the womb of a woman.

Colossians 1:16 begins with this phrase: *"For by Him were all things created."* That displays the divinity of Jesus. He was present at the creation of the world.

For by him were all things created, that are in heaven, and that are in earth, visible and invisible,

> **whether they be thrones, or dominions, or princi-
> palities, or powers: all things were created by him,
> and for him: And he is before all things, and by him
> all things consist. And he is the head of the body, the
> church: who is the beginning, the firstborn from the
> dead; that in all things he might have the
> preeminence.**
>
> **(Col. 1:16-18)**

There is that word *"firstborn"* again. This is even a stranger statement than the first. How can anyone be born from the dead? I read in the Bible where Jesus raised people from the dead. I read where Jesus himself was resurrected from the dead, but I do not find anything about people being born from the dead — except when it has to do with spiritual rebirth.

When a man is born again, he passes from spiritual death into spiritual life. The only place in the Bible where the terminology "born from the dead" is used is when spiritual rebirth is involved.

Could it be that Jesus was born again from spiritual death and became the head of the Body of Christ? If that is true, then there had to be a time when Jesus was spiritually dead in order for Him to be born again from the dead.

In Revelation 1:5, Jesus is called *"the first begotten of the dead."* Since He raised people from the dead *before* His own resurrection, that cannot be referring to physical resurrection.

Romans 8:29 says that we who have accepted Christ as our Savior are part of the family of God, and Jesus is referred to as the *"firstborn,"* which makes Him our elder brother.

Paul continues in this verse (Rom. 8:29) by revealing that God foreknew we would choose Him, so He predestined us to be conformed to the image of Christ, that He might be the first among many brethren.

When some people first hear this, they think you are implying that Jesus was a sinner, who *needed* to be born again. THAT IS NOT TRUE!

We are the brothers of Christ. How did we become His brothers? We became His brothers by being born again. So if He is the firstborn, then He must have been born again from spiritual death into spiritual life. Therefore, there must have been a point at which He was spiritually dead.

In Acts 2:22-39, the Apostle Peter's words on the Day of Pentecost are recorded. Peter quoted a Psalm of David that was prophetic of the Messiah. Verse 27 is from Psalm 16, the 10th verse:

> **For thou wilt not leave my soul in hell; neither wilt thou suffer thine Holy One to see corruption.**

The word translated *hell* is really a Greek word that should be translated *Hades*, the place of the departed spirits of the dead.

When humans die, only their physical bodies die. All people, who are spirits, living in bodies, go to whatever place their decisions regarding Jesus cause them to go. Christians go straight to heaven to be with the Lord. Unbelievers go downward into the earth to a place called *Hades* to be held in torment until the final judgment. At the judgment, those people will be sentenced to the lake of fire forever, there to join Satan, the one for whom hell was created.

How did Jesus wind up in Hades? He got there, not because He sinned, but because He *became* sin in our place. Jesus never sinned (Heb. 4:15), but He *became* sin. Jesus became the sacrificial Lamb on our behalf.

He became sin voluntarily because He loved us. When He became sin, He had to die. Before that, death had no claim on Him. Being born of a virgin, He had none of the sins of the earthly parents imparted to Him through inheritance. He had to lay down His life of His own free will.

The Ministry of Reconciliation

Second Corinthians 5:17,18 tells us that God reconciled us to himself by Jesus Christ and then gave us the *ministry of reconciliation.*

God is not out to condemn you. God is not the one who is telling you you are worthless. It is the devil who is telling you those lies. God knows what and who you are and where you have been, but God's desire and purpose is to reconcile you to himself.

Some people criticize me for not talking a lot about sin and about living right. Why should I spend an hour telling people not to do something that they already know not to do. Most unbelievers have an awareness of sin and know there is something wrong with it.

The light of God, your conscience (the voice of your spirit), is there to let you know when things are wrong. The Gospel is not designed to beat you down and make you feel like a "good-for-nothing" worm. God is in the business of reconciling. And the message of the Church should be a message of love and grace, not a message of condemnation.

On the other hand, that does not mean that sin should be overlooked. If someone sins, and it is our responsibility to point this out, we should do so. If it is not our responsibility to correct him, we should pray for that person. But we do not need to spend all of our time dwelling on sin.

We need to tell sinners the *good* news. Man has been reconciled to God through His Son, Jesus Christ. God has sent Jesus to make you a brand-new person, if you will only receive the paid-for redemption.

> **To wit, that God was in Christ, reconciling the world unto himself, not imputing their trespasses unto them; and hath committed unto us the word of reconciliation. Now then we are ambassadors for Christ, as though God did beseech you by us: we pray you in Christ's stead, be ye reconciled to God.**
> **(2 Cor. 5:19,20)**

Can you see it? His life and death on earth were not against Jesus' will. He was willing to do that for us. God made Him to be sin and then judged sin. God's judging of sin allows us to be made free *if* by faith we accept Christ's sacrifice of himself on our behalf.

If you and I say yes to Jesus, God gives us credit for having actually died ourselves. However, Jesus did it for us. What He did becomes ours, sets us free from the power of darkness and reconciles us to God.

Why? *That we might be made the righteousness of God in him* (2 Cor. 5:21).

The way God set up His plan is that everyone is placed on the same level. No one is better than anyone else. I do not have to be a doctor of letters to make it into the Kingdom. I do not have to be a millionaire, a great poet, a statesman or a lawyer to be called a child of God.

I do not have to have a wonderful voice to be counted important to the Lord. I do not have to be the best football player or the fastest runner. I do not have to be eloquent in my speech. But if I have the love of God in me, if I have accepted Jesus as my Savior, I am saved and I am a child of the King. Praise the Lord!

Thank God that He made His grace available for ordinary people. You can be in the "Who's Who" of heaven. Your name can be in the Lamb's Book of Life, although you may not be counted as anything here on earth.

You and I can be listed in God's book — the most important book of all!

For it pleased the Father that in him should all fulness dwell; And, having made peace through the blood of his cross, by him to reconcile all things unto himself; by him, I say, whether they be things in earth, or things in heaven.

(Col. 1:19,20)

Jesus *is* Lord of all things and all believers!

3

Jesus, the Reconciler
(Col. 1:21-26)

**And you, that were sometime alienated and
enemies in your mind by wicked works, yet now hath
he reconciled. In the body of his flesh through death,
to present you holy and unblameable and unreprove-
able in his sight.**

(Col. 1:21,22)

Remember? Verse 20 said that God made peace
through the blood and the cross of Jesus in order for
Jesus to *reconcile all things* unto himself. ''All things''
include everything in earth or heaven (v. 20b).

Then Paul continued, *''And you, that were sometime*
[at one time] *alienated...* (v. 21). How were you and
I and all men alienated? We were separated from God
by sin. We were enemies of God in our minds because
of wicked works. We were unregenerate. We had
received and inherited Adam's sin nature, and that
caused us to be separated from God, having no
communion or fellowship with Him.

How were we reconciled *in the body of His flesh
through death?* In other words, Jesus — a spirit with a
soul and body — had to leave His physical body and
go into the pit of Hades itself to serve our sentence.

Jesus' body remained in the grave while He (the spirit and soul parts of Him) went into Hades.

He did this in order to present us *holy, unblameable* and *unreprovable* in God's sight. But there is a very important condition attached to this: *"If ye continue in the faith grounded and settled"* (v. 23a).

Earlier, we talked about Christians being told to *present* (offer up) their bodies as living sacrifices. Here, Jesus wants to present *us* (offer us up) to God. We need to find out what the condition, *"if we continue in the faith,"* is all about.

The very fact that Paul said, *"If* you continue in the faith," means it is possible for you not to do so. There is a doctrine called *eternal security*, which basically means, "once saved, always saved."

There *is* eternal security — if you stay *in* Christ. No one can take you out. No one can steal your salvation. God will not let you go. However, I believe the Word teaches that it is possible to forfeit your salvation, or to give it up. But that would be no accident. That would have to be done on purpose, an act of your will.

"Losing your salvation" would have to be a volitional, deliberate, calculated, premeditated act of your will, a decision to repudiate Christ knowingly. If I cannot give up my salvation, then why would Paul say *if you continue in the faith?*

How did you get saved in the first place? How did you become a Christian? How did you become a child of God? How did you get your name in the Lamb's Book of Life? You did it by receiving Jesus *by faith*.

Jesus was, and is a gift from God to the world. Therefore, salvation is a gift. There is only one way to obtain a gift, and that is to receive it. You cannot buy it. You cannot earn it. There is nothing you can do to become worthy of it.

The moment you buy something, earn something, work hard to become "good enough" to get it, it ceases to be a gift. It becomes a reward for works or a form of payment, such as a salary.

Therefore, if you did not earn your salvation by doing some works, then *you cannot lose it by works.* Somehow we believe the blood of Jesus is powerful enough to save us, but not powerful enough to keep us. We believe we receive salvation as a gift, but we can lose it through works!

Works are irrelevant and immaterial. As a matter of fact, you do not go to hell because of your sins (evil works) anymore than you go to heaven because of your good works. *Your destination is hell if and because you refused to receive the gift of Jesus Christ that God sent to earth to reconcile you with.*

Your final and eternal destination is dependent on only one thing: what you choose to do with Jesus, your Reconciler.

There are two things you do with a gift — receive it or give it back. Suppose I asked a friend to give me his Bible because I liked it, and he willingly and gladly gave it to me as a gift with no charge whatsoever.

Then suppose that sometime later I do not want that Bible any longer. I decide that I do not want it in my house, my car or my library.

I say to my friend, ''I don't want this Bible. You can have it back. I repudiate it as a gift. I don't want anything to do with it ever again.''

If you were to repudiate Jesus knowingly, cold-bloodedly and calculatedly, knowing exactly what you were doing, that would be ''the sin unto death,'' the point of no return. But there are certain qualifications necessary before you could commit the sin unto spiritual death.

There are not many Christians, compared to the total number of those who are born again, who could commit this sin.

> **If any man see his brother sin a sin which is not unto death, he shall ask, and he shall give him life for them that sin not unto death. There is a sin unto death: I do not say that he shall pray for it.**
> **(1 John 5:16)**

If someone has committed the sin unto death, you have to forget him or her. There is nothing you can do. You cannot pray for them. *In fact, the Bible says not to pray.*

The Sin Unto Death and the Unpardonable Sin

The sin unto death is *not* the unpardonable sin. People get the two mixed up. The unpardonable sin is one that sinners commit. The sin unto death can only be committed by believers who have good knowledge and understanding of what they are doing.

When one blasphemes against the Holy Spirit, there is no forgiveness. This is considered the unpardonable sin.

> **Verily I say unto you, All sins shall be forgiven unto the sons of men, and blasphemies wheresoever they shall blaspheme: But he that shall blaspheme against the Holy Ghost hath never forgiveness, but is in danger of eternal damnation.**
> **(Mark 3:28, 29)**

Blaspheming against the Holy Spirit is denying the Holy Spirit's witness concerning Jesus being our Lord and Savior. In other words, it is like shaking your finger in the face of God and saying, ''I will not accept Jesus as my Savior. I will not acknowledge Him as Lord of my life.''

Do that enough times, and you may not get another chance.

Also attributing to the devil what the Holy Spirit is doing is dangerous. That is what the Scribes and Pharisees were doing that brought the above comment from Jesus. He was warning them they were on dangerous ground because they were saying Jesus had an unclean spirit and was doing His signs and wonders by Beelzebub (Mark 3:30).

Sometimes, demons put fear on Christians by telling them they have committed this sin. But if you are concerned about it, you have not done it! When a person commits the unpardonable sin, that person has no desire for Jesus. He or she will not care — and certainly not be worried — about committing this sin.

Who are those that can commit the unpardonable sin? As I said before, they are those people who don't really know Jesus, don't want to know Him and don't intend to know Him, even though they have been told of the necessity for receiving Him as Savior and Lord in order to be saved.

Romans 10:9 says you receive Jesus by confessing with your mouth that Jesus is Lord and by believing in your heart that God raised Him from the dead. Nothing in that verse says anything about works. Consequently, the unpardonable sin has nothing to do with sins or works.

I have heard people say, "Suppose someone accepts Christ, and lives the Christian life for a while. Then he starts yielding to the flesh or the devil and goes back out into the world, living a sinful life again."

That is sad and certainly too bad, but it is not the unpardonable sin nor is it the sin unto death.

Then someone might say, "Well, that means you can accept Jesus and live anyway you want."

I am glad I never said or thought that! A person who believes that is playing games with God. People who are for real do not accept Jesus on Monday, and go back on Tuesday to live the rest of the time in the world. That tells me there probably was never a real conversion in their lives in the first place.

However, sometimes people are not taught the Word. They are born again, but they are in a church situation where people are not taught to walk in faith. These people never learn how to become victorious Christians. They are constantly up and down like a yo-yo. They live in and out of sin, in and out of this, that and the other thing.

But always they have something on the inside of them that keeps tugging at their consciences, and that is the Holy Spirit. They may repent 999 times, then go right back out and do the same thing again. They do not know how to take advantage of their covenant rights.

What they are really doing is living defeated Christian lives. Their witness for Jesus is no good because of their life-styles. They cannot tell anyone about Jesus, because no one would believe they know Him.

Satan is able to keep them in sickness and disease, poverty and fear. But their names are still written in the Lamb's Book of Life, and they will go to heaven, *because no one goes to heaven on his or her good works.*

This one point would help so many people to understand God's ways and plans: *You are not born again, nor do you get to heaven, because of good works. Conversely, you do not go to hell because of bad works. What sends people to hell is the rejection of Jesus and His redemptive work done at Calvary.*

You will get rewards for good works, but salvation comes by faith through accepting Jesus as your Savior. I have taken a good bit of space to discuss this, but it is a much-misunderstood and very important subject.

You cannot go by outward appearances. Some people may fool you with an angelic look or fool the preacher with their ''Bible-toting,'' ''Holy Spirit-acting'' ways. But no one is going to get away with anything with God.

Do not worry about anyone slipping something over on God. No one is going to pull anything on Him. He knows the hearts of men. The wheels of divine justice grind ever so slowly — and all of us can be thankful for that — but those wheels do grind ever so finely.

God Looks at the Heart!

When God gets through sifting out the chaff, it will be dust for the wind to drive away. If someone is not living right, God knows his heart. Jesus died for that man or woman. You did not, so do not worry about other people's salvation. Pray for them, witness to them if the Holy Spirit moves you to do so, but spend more time seeking God about your own testimony and life-style.

The sin unto death is committed when someone uses the same mouth that confessed Jesus as Lord and Savior to say, ''I don't want this man Jesus any longer to have anything to do with me. I repudiate Him. He is not my Savior. He is not my Lord. I want nothing to do with Him ever again.''

But that person has to be a completely mature and experienced Christian to be guilty of that. When you know a lot spiritually, you are held accountable for what you know. You must be experienced in the Word.

Baby Christians can never be guilty of the sin unto death. Some Christians have been saved twenty-five years or longer, but they are still babies. You can tell babies, because they are always crying about someone taking advantage of them. They are petty, jealous, full of strife, gossipers, fault-finders and they are easily offended.

They have not come to know how to walk in faith and walk by the Word. Hebrews 6 lists the criteria for those who can commit the sin unto death:

> **Therefore leaving the principles of the doctrine of Christ, let us go on unto perfection; not laying again the foundation of repentance from dead works, and of faith toward God. Of the doctrine of baptisms, and of laying on of hands, and of resurrection of the dead, and of eternal judgment. And this will we do, if God permit. For it is impossible for those who were once enlightened, and have tasted of the heavenly gift, and were made partakers of the Holy Ghost. And have tasted the good word of God, and the powers of the world to come. If they shall fall away, to renew them again unto repentance; seeing they crucify to themselves the Son of God afresh, and put him to an open shame.**
>
> **(Heb. 6:1-6)**

You would have to have all of those things working against you in order to even qualify for committing the sin unto death. Let's look at these qualifiers a little closer:

(1) You have to be once enlightened.

(2) You have to have tasted the heavenly gift.

(3) You have to have been a partaker of the Holy Spirit.

(4) You have to have tasted the good Word of God.

(5) You have to be operating in the powers of the world to come (moving in the gifts of the Spirit).

You can tell from this how few people are really in a position to commit the sin unto death.

Sometimes Christians who have been walking with Jesus for a little while begin to feel pressure from spouses, relatives or friends. The dog, cat and bumble bee are "on their case" about being a Christian.

They may get so frustrated that they throw up their hands and say, "I wish I'd never heard of Jesus! I'm sorry I ever became a Christian!"

All of us have heard of situations like that. But do you know what God does with those people? He does the same thing you would do if you had a three-year-old who fell in the middle of the kitchen floor and yelled, "I hate you! I hate you!" because you would not give him any more cookies.

How much attention do you pay to that? Most mothers just ignore such a situation. They let the yelling go in one ear and out the other, because they know a child that age does not understand what he is saying.

But when a twenty-one-year-old child stands in front of his parent and says, "I hate you," trouble is brewing. He *knows* what he is saying.

So, for all intents and purposes, in the majority of cases, "once saved, always saved" is true.

Colossians 1:23 tells us how *to continue in the faith:*

**If ye continue in the faith grounded and settled,
and be not moved away from the hope of the gospel,**

which ye have heard, and which was preached to every creature which is under heaven; whereof I Paul am made a minister.

If you are "grounded and settled," you can continue in the faith, Paul said. However, many Christians are not grounded and settled. That is the way babies are, happy one day and crying the next.

If you are having trouble along this line, let me tell you how to get grounded and settled. You do it by learning the Word of God. That will keep you from being moved by every wind of doctrine that comes up. You will be standing solid on the Word of God.

Let the winds blow, and the clouds gather, you can stand in the eye of the storm and say, "In the name of Jesus, peace be still."

When you are a baby Christian, you tend to fall apart when a storm arises. But someone who is grounded and settled on the Word will not be moved.

Why tell us to *"be not moved away from the hope of the gospel"* if there were no danger of being moved away? Why even mention it? The very fact that Paul felt it necessary to write this to the Colossians proves that they, and we today, *could* be moved.

One problem in the Church down through the ages has been "self-made" ministers. Paul said, *"...whereof I Paul am made a minister."* Paul did not say he had decided to become a minister, or that he had made himself one.

Too many ministers are self-made, or parent-made or spouse-made and, consequently, they have no anointing. Many ministers go to seminaries to get degrees for careers in the ministry. They believe the degree *makes* them a minister, but that is not true. Wait for God to make you a minister. Then your ministry will bear fruit.

Paul says:

> **Who now rejoice in my sufferings for you, and fill up that which is behind of the afflictions of Christ in my flesh for his body's sake, which is the church: Whereof I am made a minister, according to the dispensation of God which is given to me for you, to fulfil the word of God: Even the mystery which hath been hid from ages and from generations, but now is made manifest to his saints.**
> **(Col. 1:24-26)**

The Greek word translated *sufferings*[5] in verse 24 literally means, "while I am enduring and in the midst of the tribulations and the persecutions that Satan is bringing against me."

God does not ask us to enjoy hurting and being in pain. But as long as Satan is in this world, you are going to have to put up with tribulations, temptations, trials, fears and persecutions. But you can be an overcomer through all of it.

Being *grounded and settled* means being able to live a victorious life.

What did Paul mean by *the afflictions of Christ*? Some people have the mistaken idea that we are to be

---

[5]*Wuest's Word Studies from the Greek New Testament for the English Reader,* Volume One; Page 191 by Kenneth S. Wuest, Wm.B. Eerdmans Publishing Company Reprinted, March, 1978.

nailed to a cross. But Jesus never asked us to take up *His* cross. It would not do anyone any good for you or me to be nailed to a cross.

What Paul meant was for us to take up the commitment we made to Jesus and to understand that we have to put up with the same things Jesus did. Those things range from being misunderstood by your family and friends to being made fun of at work for your life-style and testimony. In some places in nearly every generation, *taking up your cross* (Matt. 16:24) and *the afflictions of Christ* (Col. 1:24) have meant literal persecution.

Jesus' own family and friends did not understand who He was in the beginning of His ministry. They thought He had ''gone off the deep end!'' (Mark 3:21; John 7:3-5.) His countrymen, especially the religious leaders of His day, tried to discredit Him and entrap Him, and finally they had Him killed, but He overcame all of those afflictions and taught us that we can also.

Called for the Benefit of the Body

Paul said he was enduring all of this in his flesh (in reality) *''for the Church's sake''* (v. 24). He was rejoicing in the things he was undergoing for the sake of the Body of Christ. The words *''in my sufferings''* literally mean:

> **In the midst of all of the trials and tribulations, and while Satan is bringing all of this persecution against me, I am rejoicing for you and for the Body of Christ. I rejoice to be counted worthy to suffer shame and persecution for the Word's sake.**

Again, in verse 25, Paul repeated those words *"...whereof I am made a minister."* When God calls a man and places His anointing on that man, He does not call him for the sake of the *man*. God calls people for His purposes and for the sake of the body of believers.

God did not call me to preach to me. He called me to preach and teach and pastor a portion of the Body of Christ. When you are called into one of the five-fold offices, Satan comes against you in a different way than he does the layman.

Because ministers affect a lot of people, they come under greater attacks than other believers. I believe Paul repeated the fact that he had been *made* a minister because it is an important point. As I said before, Paul did not make himself a minister. Bible schools and seminaries do not make ministers — they only teach them.

God calls you, then shapes, forms and molds you into the ministry gift He wants you to be — as much as you will let Him. God has to do that. You cannot take it upon yourself to be called into the ministry. Being God's spokesman is an awesome responsibility.

Paul was saying that God had made him accountable for the stewardship of preaching the Gospel. The *mystery* of which he speaks in verse 26 *is* the good news (gospel) that God has reconciled man to himself in the person of Jesus Christ.

The Holy Spirit had inspired prophets and writers through the years who wrote prophetic statements about the Messiah. Until Jesus actually came and worked out the fulfillment of God's plan, no one really understood those words about the Messiah. Their meanings had been "hidden" throughout ages and generations, although looking back at the Old Testament now, God's plan seems clear to us.

But, Paul said, *now* we can understand. Now what God was *really* saying is revealed. But you must be a *saint* (v. 26) for it to be revealed to you. *Saint* simply means "a born-again child of God." The natural mind (of unbelievers) cannot understand the things of the spirit (1 Cor. 2:14).

This truth is made a littler clearer in Paul's Letter to the Ephesians.

> **For this cause I Paul, the prisoner of Jesus Christ for you Gentiles, If ye have heard of the dispensation of the grace of God which is given me to you-ward: How that by revelation he made known unto me the mystery; (as I wrote afore in few words, Whereby, when ye read, ye may understand my knowledge in the mystery of Christ) Which in other ages was not made known unto the sons of men, as it is now revealed unto his holy apostles and prophets by the Spirit; That the Gentiles should be fellowheirs, and of the same body, and partakers of his promise in Christ by the gospel: Whereof I was made a minister, according to the gift of the grace of God given unto me by the effectual working of his power.**
>
> **(Eph. 3:1-7)**

In these verses, Paul is saying almost the same thing that he states in Colossians 1:25,26. However, here in Ephesians, he clarifies a couple of things. He lets us know that this "mystery" is *in* Jesus Christ. Unless you are *in* Christ, you will never be able to comprehend, know and understand the truth of the Word of God. The Bible always will be a mystery to you.

The Old Testament (Old Covenant) was sort of a "promissory note," a "credit card" on what was coming later. They had prophetic words; and, also, examples were given through the recorded lives of men and women of the past, but the truth could not be wholly understood until it happened.

Isaac was the natural son of promise to Abraham; Jesus is the *real* Son of Promise (Gal. 3:16). The natural always is a shadow which disappears, and the spiritual is the reality which lasts forever (2 Cor. 4:18).

The sacrifices under the Old Covenant were natural animals. But Jesus was the spiritual sacrifice under the New Covenant — *"the lamb of God, which taketh away the sin of the world"* (John 1:29). But what the sacrifices really meant was a mystery until *after* the Crucifixion. The "saints" (Rom. 1:7), as believers are called in the New Testament, could understand *"the mystery which hath been hid from ages and from generations"* (Col. 1:26).

But in Paul's day, and in all generations since, the mystery is not "hidden," but it *"is made manifest to his saints"* (v. 26).

4
Jesus, the Dweller Within
(Col. 1:27-29)

To whom God would make known what is the riches of the glory of this mystery among the Gentiles; which is Christ in you, the hope of glory; Whom we preach, warning every man, and teaching every man in all wisdom; that we may present every man perfect in Christ Jesus: Whereunto I also labour, striving according to his working, which worketh in me mightily.

(Col. 1:27-29)

For years, I had a difficult time understanding Christ *in* me. I would read the Bible, memorize those verses, and even quote them, but I never had any comprehension of what this phrase meant. How is Christ in me?

Paul said believers in general (of whom the believers at Colossae were a specific group) were the ones to whom God wanted to make known the riches of His glory. And the riches of his glory is *Christ in you, the hope of glory.*

Physically speaking, Jesus is in heaven. At the end of Acts 7, Stephen was being stoned to death (vv. 58-60). Just before this, he looked up and saw Jesus

51

standing at the right hand of the Father (v. 55). Jesus was not on earth, but in heaven at the right hand of the Father. So how can He be in me and you and in heaven at the same time?

Unfortunately, many Christians do not understand this biblical truth. But what all of the theological discussions boil down to is this: Christ is in you *by faith.* To the degree that you operate in faith, to that degree you are going to experience the reality of Christ in you.

The bigger your faith, the larger your concept of Christ in you is going to be. Too many Christians look to a miniature-sized Jesus because of their lack of faith.

We need to become God-inside minded. Jesus is not just "out there, somewhere." He lives within the *real* you, the spirit within your body. The temple of God today is a Christian's body.

God is not in a building. He is not in that cathedral on the corner with a big gold cross on top, unless Christians go into that building, taking God with them. God is in those of us who have allowed Him to come in and to make His habitation inside of us. *God lives in you.*

That is part of this "mystery" about which Paul writes. You are able to comprehend it by faith alone.

I am not talking about the esoteric idea that "God is in all of us, a divine spark of life." That is New Age garbage. God dwells only within those who have accepted His Son Jesus as their Savior and Lord.

If you do not understand how to walk by faith, your concepts of Jesus and of the Father are not going to be very high. Most Christians cannot rely on God enough because they cannot develop trust in a God who is not real. If He were real to us, it would be exceedingly difficult for us to sin.

If a Christian *really* believed God lived within him, it would be very difficult for him to get involved in some of the things that have made headline news in recent years.

With the concept of God way off in the heavens somewhere, a person might think, "Well, I'll just pull down the blinds, throw the covers over my head, and God will not know what is going on."

But we need to understand that God is with us all the time. However, we need to know *how* He is with us. As I said earlier, in previous years, I had a problem with the things of God, because it seemed He was way off somewhere in the distance. He seemed so far away that He was not truly real to me.

I would work myself up into some kind of a spiritual feeling and say, "Boy, the disciples were blessed to have Jesus walking and talking with them. They were so fortunate to have a chance to see Him and actually touch Him. Just think about that, touching Jesus on a daily basis, being able to listen to His words, look into His eyes and really watch Him performing miracles.

But we are almost 2,000 years removed from those days. So, how do we relate to Him now?

Many times I felt hypocritical, acting as if Jesus and God were with me when I could not see, touch or talk to them face to face. My problem was attempting to figure out mentally how God was with me and how I could relate to Christ.

I had this childish idea that there might be a miniature Jesus seated on the inside of me, but He was so small that He had no real effect on my life. However, one day, I found out exactly how it all operates.

That Christ May Dwell in Your Heart

First, you need to be sure you have repented of your past life, turned to God through Christ and accepted Jesus as your personal Savior. For a better understanding, look again at Paul's Letter to the Ephesians.

> **Whereof I was made a minister, according to the gift of the grace of God given unto me by the effectual working of his power. Unto me, who am less than the least of all saints, is this grace given, that I should preach among the Gentiles the unsearchable riches of Christ; And to make all men see what is the fellowship of the mystery, which from the beginning of the world hath been hid in God, who created all things by Jesus Christ: To the intent that now unto the principalities and powers in heavenly places might be known by the church the manifold wisdom of God. According to the eternal purpose which he purposed in Christ Jesus our Lord: In whom we have boldness and access with confidence by the faith of him. Wherefore I desire that ye faint not at my tribulations for you, which is your glory. For this cause I bow my knees unto the Father of our Lord Jesus Christ, Of whom the whole family in heaven and earth is named, That he would grant you, according to the riches of his glory, to be strengthened with might by his Spirit in the inner man. That Christ**

**may dwell in your hearts by faith; that ye, being
rooted and grounded in love, May be able to
comprehend with all saints what is the breadth, and
length, and depth, and height; And to know the love
of Christ, which passeth knowledge, that ye might be
filled with all the fulness of God. Now unto him that
is able to do exceeding abundantly above all that we
ask or think, according to the power that worketh in
us, Unto him be glory in the church by Christ Jesus
throughout all ages, world without end. Amen.**

(Eph. 3:7-21)

Ephesians 3:17 says, "That Christ may dwell in
your hearts *by faith.*" The word *dwell* in that verse is
a very "pregnant" word in the Greek, a word that
gives birth to many facets of understanding. The Greek
word *katoikeo* properly signifies "to settle down in a
dwelling, to dwell fixedly in a place," according to
Vine's Expository Dictionary.

Vine's Expository Dictionary also says that, in
addition to its literal sense, this word is used of "the
indwelling of the totality of the attributes and powers
of the Godhead in Christ" (Col. 1:19; 2:9) . . . "the
indwelling of Christ in the hearts of believers" (Eph.
3:17), and "the future indwelling of righteousness in
the new heavens and earth" (2 Pet. 3:13).[6]

Therefore, we can see that when Paul talked of
Christ dwelling in us, he was referring to a permanent
situation, not temporary or sometimes, but all the time,
forever. Christ is not making an "overnight" visit to

[6]Vine's, Vol. 1, p. 345.

your heart, but through the Holy Spirit, He puts down roots and transforms you into a fit dwelling for himself.

Notice that in Ephesians 3:17, Paul said Christ dwells in us, while in Colossians 1:19 — which we studied in chapter two of this book — Paul said *all fullness* dwells in Christ. That means He is in us *permanently* and all things are *in* Him forever.

However, Paul said that Christ *may* dwell in our hearts *by faith. May* implies permission. Christ *may* dwell in our hearts *if we let Him.* Each believer has a part in this process of becoming one with Christ, and that is a very simple part: receiving Him into your heart, giving Him permission to dwell within you. *You* are responsible for giving permission.

So Jesus is not faraway, off in the heavens, and He is not a miniature figure of some kind in you. He not only fills you up, but He is *with* you. He sees everything you see, hears everything you say, knows everything you think. He knows everything you do while you are doing it!

Walking by Faith, not by Sight

You can pull down the shades, but when you get into bed, He is there. You might as well have left the shades up if you are trying to hide what you do from Jesus.

To the degree that you understand this principle of Christ being in you by faith, to that degree your life will be changed. This revelation will change your way of thinking, change the way you act, and it will have a tremendous positive effect on your life.

Some cars used to be manufactured with a "governor" on their engines. You could only drive such a car so fast. No matter how hard you pressed the accelerator to the floor, the car would only go forty-five miles an hour.

Understanding that Jesus is within you will act as a "governor" on your life. That understanding will keep you from getting into many things that you might otherwise slip or fall into.

Now, *Jesus* will not stop you from doing those things. He has been within you since you became born again, and He has not stopped you living according to the world, has He? He has not *made* you change your life-style, because He will not overrule your will.

Every human, believer and non-believer alike, has the right to make his own choices. *Knowing* that Jesus *is* with you everywhere you go and that He sees everything you think and do gives you the incentive to make the right choices. He is not there to spy on you. He is *part* of you, and you are *part* of Him. You cannot remain a born-again child of God and not have Jesus go with you wherever you go.

He will help you be the best you can be, a real man or a real woman of God. He will help you become a person of integrity, a person who lives a godly life-style. However, you have to *believe* that He is within you, or you may not make the right choices.

This understanding has nothing to do with feelings. Do not judge anything or base anything on feelings and emotions. If you do, then what happens when you do not "feel" as if Jesus is in you? Did He leave? Of course not. Your feelings changed for some reason, but Jesus does not change.

I am so glad I was "delivered" from being moved by feelings. There was a time when I thought God was not with me, and I was not spiritual, because I could not get my feelings in line with my beliefs. I would sit in church and try with all my might to work up some tears, because I thought tears showed spirituality.

I did not understand that anytime you cry, you will feel better. Crying is an emotional release, like letting steam out of a tea kettle. Unfortunately, some people have interpreted feeling better after crying in church as a spiritual experience. Actually, it is an emotional experience.

In the church I attended at that time, crying was easy with the kind of songs we sang. By the time we got through, it was easy to cry. Then I would feel good, because I had had an emotional release.

But on Monday morning, I was right back in the dumps — whipped, defeated, scared and no more mature as a Christian than I was before I went to church. I have found that God's Word is the thing that will never let you down. His Word is the same, no matter what or how you feel.

When you learn to make your confessions about life based on the Word of God, you will never have another problem with feelings. I can be bold — not because I feel like it — but because the Word encourages me to be bold. I can be bold because *"greater is He that is in you [me], than he that is in the world!"* (1 John 4:4).

I found out walking by faith and not by sight (2 Cor. 5:7) eliminates a lot of problems as well as a lot of stress and anxiety. This kind of walk frees you from the circumstances. The devil is stirring up circumstances all the time. There is never a time when nothing is going on to pull you down.

Either the cat ate the canary, or the fence fell down, or your tires are flat, or the company you work for is going out of business. *Something* is going on to keep you off balance all of the time. Walking by sight enables the devil to keep you trapped in circumstances.

Can you imagine what it is like being the pastor of a large church? Can you imagine what it is like to listen to people's problems all day long? In the natural, pastoring is enough to put you under. I know some ministers who tried to handle their calling in the natural and actually did go under.

People will drive you up the wall, through the wall and out the other side of the wall! But when you walk by faith, you rise above all of the problems, the stress and the busy schedule. I am not saying I do not have a chance to react to circumstances. But I am saying that I do not allow negative things to affect me.

I found out how to love the Lord and how to trust Him, and that freed me from the hang-up of emotions and feelings.

People say to me, "Oh, Brother Price, I wish I had what you have."

And I answer, "You do! You are just not operating in it. That's all that is wrong."

They say, "You just don't know how hard it is to operate by faith."

My reply is, ''No! It is *not* hard to operate by faith. What is hard is making up your mind that you are going to live that way. Once you make a quality decision to live by faith, the living-it-out part is not hard.''

The only way you will ever know if God's Word is true is to trust His Word and to put it into operation. I proved my faith through tithes and offerings. I could argue about whether the Word is true until I turn blue in the face, but I won't know if it is or not until I do it.

You will not know whether the man you work for will really pay you until you work a week or sometimes two weeks, and find out for sure. So I began paying the tithe to a God that I could not see, a Jesus I could not touch. I proved *by faith* that the Word was true. Ten-percent giving worked so well that I went up to twenty-five percent. I found that the more I give, the more I receive.

I am not giving just to receive, but I am into the flow of the principle of sowing and reaping, giving and receiving and the principle is working.

Christ in You, the Hope of Glory

The same principle of faith works as well when it comes to loving God as it does in giving.

John 14:15 says that if you love God, you will keep His commandments. That is not talking about the Ten Commandments only. Jesus was talking about the Word of God, and He has told us more than ten things to do.

Jesus said that *if* we loved Him, we would *keep* His words, and the Father would love us.

> **If a man love me, he will keep my words: and my Father will love him, and will come unto him, and make our abode with him. He that loveth me not keepeth not my sayings: and the word which ye hear is not mine, but the Father's which sent me.**
> **(John 14:23,24)**

When I really read those verses, I said, "Hallelujah, I am free! I am free!" I found out how to love the Father: Keep His Word. *Keep* means *to do* His Word. All I have to do to show God that I love Him is to study the Word and do whatever it tells me to.

I do not keep His Word to *earn* His love, because His love is a free gift. But by keeping His Word, by hearing and willingly obeying, I can show the Father that I love Him. He showed that He loved me when He sent Jesus to Calvary (John 3:16).

Why was Paul writing these things to these people? Verse 28 says his desire was to *"present every man perfect in Christ Jesus."* Paul said that was why he labored, working in the Church as Jesus worked mightily in him (v. 29).

Perfect in verse 28 does not mean "flawless," as it does to us today. It means "mature, fully grown, or fully developed." How does God bring people to spiritual maturity? How does He *perfect* us?

Jesus placed ministry gifts in the Church in order to perfect the saints.

> **And he gave some, apostles; and some, prophets; and some, evangelists; and some, pastors and teachers; For the perfecting of the saints, for the work of the ministry, for the edifying of the body of Christ.**
> **(Eph. 4:11,12)**

Through the ministry gifts, the people of God are to be taught the Word and brought to maturity in the things of God. The ministry gifts are not supposed to entertain people. They are not set in the Church to excite the saints, to create great emotional experiences or to make the saints feel good. Those in the five-fold offices are to *teach and train* the saints.

Literally, they are supposed to do the very same thing a school teacher does. A good school teacher is concerned about training students to make it in life. Students are to be prepared for life so that when they go out into the world, they will be able to take care of themselves and not end up being wards of the state.

When Paul said he was to *warn* every man, *teach* every man and *present* every man (Col. 1:28), he did not mean every person in the world. He meant every person in the family of God.

When I began pastoring, I was at one church for about eight and a half years. For the first five years, the people were babies. They were not growing because I was not teaching them. The "buck" stops at the pulpit. I gave a pretty good sermon every week, one that sounded good and was fairly entertaining.

I spiced up my sermons with illustrations, and I had a lot of zeal and dedication. At least my messages were not boring or dull. However, the people were not learning very much, because I was not teaching very much.

Many churches today are like mine was: a spiritual entertainment center. This is not meant as a criticism, but rather as an observation. I was guilty of this myself. Of course, the main reason I was not teaching anything was because I did not know anything!

Most people think it is very sad when a child has never had the opportunity to go to school , and they feel the same way about an adult who had the opportunity but did not use it. Can you imagine how God must feel when He sees His children go to church week after week and never grow up?

I heard someone who was criticizing today's churches, say, ''The churches are nothing but big Bible classes!''

And I thought, ''But that is what they are supposed to be!''

Tradition has convinced us that churches should be spiritual entertainment centers or evangelistic services where the minister preaches ''hell fire and brimstone.''

Christians do not need to hear evangelistic services. Save those for street preaching, tent revivals or times when large numbers of unbelievers are present. Those already born into the Kingdom of God need to learn about God's Word, His plan, His purpose and His will for their lives. They need to learn how to deal with the issues of life. Otherwise, they have wasted their time.

Who Is Responsible for Winning Souls?

Some Christians think the pastor is placed in office to get people saved. But you have never heard of a shepherd giving birth to sheep. Sheep give birth to lambs, and the shepherd is to *take care* of the sheep *and* the lambs.

Jesus sees the local church as a sheepfold, and the pastor as an undershepherd under Him, the Chief Shepherd. A pastor is to witness as he passes through the community and through life, but his main job is to cook up and serve a good nutritional meal week after week.

The pastor really is a spiritual chef, fixing food for the sheep every week. They are to eat that food, get fat on it and go out to bring in more sheep to get fed. The entire process is to be repeated until Jesus returns.

This subject is so important because people are waiting for Jesus to come back at any time. They have their bags packed, and they are sitting on the side of the road, waiting for "the Rapture bus" to come along.

I have said this before, and I might as well say it again, if it will shake some Christians out of illusion and into reality. Jesus is not coming for this motley, infantile, undernourished, immature, babified church. That is not the kind of bride for which He is returning. About ninety-nine percent of today's Christians are babies.

I did not say they did not love the Lord. I did not say they were not saved. I did not say they were not going to heaven. What I am saying is that most Christians are not grown up. God is still waiting for the churches to do what He told them to do.

Ephesians 4:1-16 is a detailed description of this principle. Paul said the ministry gifts are for the perfecting or maturing of the saints, for the work of the ministry, for the edifying or building up of the Body of Christ until *"we all come in the unity of the faith, and of the knowledge of the Son of God, unto a perfect* [mature] *man"* (Eph. 4:13).

The Church is to continue this process until Christians no longer act like children, running after every new thing that comes along. But they are to grow up into Christ in all things. Too many Christians are abdicating their responsibilities, leaving the "work of the ministry" to the pastor, the choir director, the ushers or to anyone else who is willing to serve.

Think of everyone in the Body of Christ as a link in a chain. And then you can understand that old adage, "A chain is only as strong as its weakest link." Babies are weak, and the Church today is mostly made up of weak links. We are not ready to be presented to Christ as mature children of God who are conformed to the image of Christ.

There are some who are growing, of course. There are some who are taking advantage of the teaching of the Word and who are becoming fully grown in the things of God. The only way Christians will be able to overcome the onslaught of the enemy that comes against them, collectively as the Church or individually as those called by Christ's name, is to learn to operate in the Word.

5

Jesus, Our Wisdom and Knowledge (Col. 2:1-7)

Chapter two of the Epistle to the Colossians shows clearly the Lordship of Jesus. In this chapter, Paul also deals with the false teaching of gnosticism, which he feared was beginning to be mixed with the truth about Christ.

Before the apostle got to the point of correcting these early Christians, however, he assured them that his concern was for their benefit. He was not upset because their "doctrines" did not match his teachings. His concern was for their welfare, because their "philosophical theology" was not simply a different *doctrine;* it was a teaching inspired by the devil to undermine the truth about God's plan and God's Son.

Paul wanted these Colossian believers to know that, although he had not seen them face to face, his love and concern was no less than for those Christians he *had* seen. He wanted them to be united in love and to be able to receive full understanding of the treasures of wisdom and knowledge that are hidden in Jesus.

For I would that ye knew what great conflict I have for you, and for them at Laodicea, and for as

many as have not seen my face in the flesh; That their hearts might be comforted, being knit together in love, and unto all riches of the full assurance of understanding, to the acknowledgement of the mystery of God, and of the Father, and of Christ; In whom are hid all the treasures of wisdom and knowledge.

(Col. 2:1-3)

The word *conflict* in verse 1 is the Greek word *agon*, which literally means a contest, such as in sports or games. But, spiritually, it means "the inward conflict of the soul," a result of anxiety over something. Paul was really *anxious* over their spiritual welfare.[7]

And in verse 2, he uses that word *mystery* again. This seems to be one of Paul's favorite words — the one he felt best fitted the explanation of something that can only be understood by the Spirit of God.

A *mystery* is not something that cannot be solved; it is only unknown to you because you do not understand it at a particular time. In order to get understanding about any of the things of God, you must first spend time searching and studying the Scriptures. Then you must spend time praying in the Spirit to build yourself up and to cause yourself to become sensitive enough to the Holy Spirit to hear Him when He gives you the revelation.

A person who does not make a dedicated effort to spend time studying the Word, line upon line and precept upon precept (Isa. 28:10) will find that the Bible

---

[7]Vine's, Vol. 1, p. 226.

will *remain* a mystery. What good does it do God, or us, to give us instructions that we cannot understand? God does not intend for His Word to be a mystery to us.

The Bible does not have "secret" knowledge, in the sense that only a few have the right "code" or the right "key to unvail its truths." This was one of the beliefs of gnosticism — only a group of "elite," special, above-average people could *really* understand what the Bible said.

However, God's mysteries are open to anyone who will let the Bible interpret itself and who will take the time to read, pray over what is read and study it. By "interpreting itself," I mean looking up all the other references where a certain word or subject is mentioned and seeing what it means in those contexts.

Today, the mystery of the Seed promised to Eve, the Son promised to Abraham, and the Descendant of David destined to rule on the throne of God's Kingdom forever and ever has been made clear. From the early church on, Christians have the best sight possible of past things. We have "hindsight." Looking back to see what happened is always clearer than looking ahead and trying to figure out what is going to happen — even from prophecies.

Paul said *all* wisdom and knowledge are hidden in Christ (v. 3). Earthly education is good, but it is not *real* education, and it is not wisdom. To be truly educated, you must be born again, filled with the Holy Spirit, and have your mind renewed with the Word to be able to hear the things of the Lord.

In verse 4, we see Paul's concern spelled out clearly.

> **And this I say, lest any man should beguile you with enticing words. For though I be absent in the flesh, yet am I with you in the spirit, joying and beholding your order, and the steadfastness of your faith in Christ.**

Operating Beyond the Natural

Some people think Paul was speaking figuratively, that he was saying, "I can't really be with you, but I am with you in thought. I'll be with you in prayer."

However, I believe he was speaking literally. I believe this spiritual giant, this mighty man of God, got into some areas of spiritual perception and awareness that are awesome. God is bigger than this universe. He is everywhere, which is beyond the human mind's ability to comprehend. I believe Paul was there with these Christians in his spirit.

Satan has a counterfeit of this phenomenon of God, and it is called "astral travel" or "soul travel." Let me tell you something: your soul is not going anywhere without *you*, the spirit-man or the spirit-woman. But God can call the real you out of your body for a visit to heaven or to show you something elsewhere on earth.

Also, on some occasions, God has transported someone — spirit, soul *and* body — to somewhere else instantly. The evangelist Philip is an example of this.

The angel of the Lord spoke to Philip and told him to leave Jerusalem and to take the road that goes into

Gaza, which was desert country. On the road, he came upon a high-ranking official of Ethiopia, who apparently was a proselyte to Judaism — one who had accepted the Jewish religion on his own rather than being born into it. Luke wrote that this man *had "come to Jerusalem for to worship"* (Acts 8:27).

At this point, he was returning to his own country. He was reading a scroll of the Book of Isaiah. The Holy Spirit told Philip to join the man, which the evangelist did. After explaining to him the passages in Isaiah that related to the Messiah, Philip got the man saved and baptized in some nearby water.

> **And when they were come up out of the water, *the Spirit of the Lord caught away Philip,* that the eunuch saw him no more: and he went on his way rejoicing. But Philip was found at Azotus: and passing through he preached in all the cities, till he came to Caesarea.**
>
> **(Acts 8:39,40, italics mine)**

The same thing, only even more of a miracle, happened to Jesus and the disciples once, according to the Gospel of John. The disciples were headed across the Sea of Galilee without Jesus when a great wind began blowing. They looked up to see Jesus walking on the water and they became afraid.

> **But he saith unto them, It is I; be not afraid. Then they willingly received him into the ship: and *immediately* the ship was at the land whither they went.**
>
> **(John 6:20,21, italics mine)**

In our day, I know of a situation where a Christian man was taken into police custody in a South American country because of his preaching of the Gospel. The police beat him almost to death and left him in solitary confinement in prison.

He said he was a "mess." He was bleeding and in a great deal of pain, but he began to pray. The man says that to this day, he does not know what happened nor does he understand it. However, suddenly, he was standing outside the prison completely well, as if he had never been beaten. So he just walked off and went about his business!

Another man and his wife were led by the Spirit of God to go to a certain place. One minute, they were standing at a railway station with their suitcases; the next minute, they were at their destination.

There are many things that many Christians have not yet started to get into, because of natural or worldly thinking. Most of the Church is operating by sight, and not by faith. And that is backwards to the Kingdom of God.

In the Book of Revelation, John talks about being *"carried...away in the spirit* into the wilderness"* (Rev. 17:3, italics mine). So when Paul said that he was *absent in the flesh, but present in the spirit,* I believe he was speaking literally. Physical death is simply a separation of the spirit and soul from the body *permanently,* that is until the Rapture takes place (1 Cor. 15:51-53). Being "caught away in the spirit" means leaving the body *temporarily.* I believe in days to come we will see more of this sort of thing happening.

An example of God using this sort of thing to uncover wickedness involved the prophet Elisha and his servant in the Old Testament (2 Kings 5). Elisha refused to take any pay for his word from God for the healing of the Syrian general, Naaman. But Elisha's servant followed the Syrian party, stopped them on the road out of Elisha's sight and pretended the prophet had changed his mind.

He asked Naaman for two suits of clothes and some silver. Then he returned to his house and went to see the prophet. When Elisha asked him where he had been, he lied and said, *"Thy servant went no whither"* (2 Kings 5:25).

This shows that a prophet does not know everything all of the time. He only knows what God chooses to show him. Otherwise, Gehazi would have expected Elisha to know everything he did. However, the servant did not think his master would know anything about what he had done.

> **And he [Elisha] said unto him, Went not mine heart with thee, when the man turned again from his chariot to meet thee? Is it a time to receive money, and to receive garments, and oliveyards, and vineyards, and sheep, and oxen, and menservants, and maidservants? The leprosy therefore of Naaman shall cleave unto thee, and unto thy seed for ever. And he [Gehazi] went out from his presence a leper as white as snow.**
>
> **(2 Kings 5:26,27)**

The Bible sometimes calls the inner man, the spirit man, the "heart."

When Elisha said, "Did my heart not go with you?" He was saying, "Did the Lord not enable me to follow you in the spirit and see this transaction of wickedness?"

You will notice, however, that before the judgment fell, the servant was given a chance to repent. If he had not lied, but had repented of a temporary lapse, he might have had to run after the Syrians and return the goods, but he would not have been judged with a penalty that would follow his descendants forever.

All Gehazi had to say was, "Oh, Master, I have messed up. I blew it and got greedy. I began to think about those new, fancy clothes and all of that gold and silver. So I thought it would not hurt to take a couple of changes of clothing and a little silver. I am so sorry. Please forgive me. Pray for God to forgive me."

However, he chose to stick with his sin and try to cover it up.

The Goal of the Christian Life

Verse 6 of Colossians 2 tells us what the Christian life is all about.

As ye have therefore received Christ Jesus the Lord, so walk ye in Him:

Many people have the idea that the goal of the Christian life is to get to heaven, but that is not true. Heaven is our literal destination, but not the goal of spiritual maturity. The goal of a Christian life is to be like Jesus.

At one time, I thought heaven was my goal. I would hear people get up in church and ask everyone to pray for them because they had been "on the King's highway a mighty long time, trying to make heaven their home."

I believe they were saying this out of sincere hearts, because that was the level of knowledge they had at the time. They thought all of the struggling in life, all of the attacks of the enemy, and persecution for the Word's sake were Satan's schemes to keep them from getting into heaven.

If you are a born-again child of God, you do not have to *try* to get to heaven. You *already* have an assurance of heaven. All you have to do to get there is to die, not struggle through life.

Satan's attacks are to try to keep you from living the victorious, overcoming life in Christ, and from doing things for God on earth. He knows he cannot keep you from heaven. But he can harass you to the point that you may not take anyone else with you!

The Christian Life Is About Being Like Jesus.

Here is where the dilemma comes, however: There are two versions of Jesus within the Church. There is the traditional religious view and then there is the Bible view. Unfortunately, the characteristics of Jesus we see in most Christians are nowhere near what the Bible decribes Him to have been when He walked the earth.

You cannot walk with someone you do not know. You cannot become like someone if you do not know what that person is like. Therefore, Paul has to be talking about the Colossians finding out who Jesus is — what He did, what He said and what He told them to do.

Also, if Paul told them to *walk in Him*, that means they were capable of doing so. God would not tell them, or us, to do something that is not within the realm of possibility. The purpose of the Word is to give us a pattern or a blueprint of what Jesus is like, and the gift of the Holy Spirit to the Church is to empower us so that we can copy His life.

If you get hung up on the religious view of Jesus, you will not even recognize the real Jesus when you see Him. The "religious" view of Jesus sees Him as a "wimp" — a guy you could push around and spit on. If that is your idea, you are a million miles off.

Jesus went where He wanted to go when He wanted to, in spite of all the opposition Satan threw at Him, directly or indirectly, through the religious leaders. He stood on the Word of His Father and accomplished the task and mission that was assigned to Him. No one or nothing was big or bad enough to stop Him.

He corrected the religious leaders many times, took a whip and ran them out of the Temple — among many other things. There has never been anyone who was more of a real man or with more strength to stick to God's purpose than Jesus.

We need to find out what the real Jesus was like and begin to copy Him. In Ephesians 4, Paul talks about the example of Jesus in contrast to the natural man given over to wickedness.

> **But ye have not so learned Christ; If so be that ye have heard him, and have been taught by him, as the truth is in Jesus: That ye put off concerning the former conversation** [King James English for *life-style*] **the old man, which is corrupt according to the deceitful lusts; But be renewed in the spirit of your mind; And that ye put on the new man, which after God is created in righteousness and true holiness.**
> **(Eph. 4:20-24)**

What we should be about as Christians is to develop and mature and grow up in the things of Christ — not to get to heaven, but to become like Jesus.

"Walk in Him" means, "Do not walk in the old ways, do not walk in the flesh."

Again, this depends on your knowing who Jesus is, and the only place where you are going to find out what He was like is in the Bible. Some people seek visions or want an angel to come and tell them about the Lord. They are wasting their time, and possibly opening themselves up to the enemy. The only place to find out accurately about Jesus is in the Word.

As you read about Jesus, the Holy Spirit will reveal Him to your spirit, and your spirit in turn will reveal Him to your mind. When you know what Jesus is really like, you can begin to copy Him, to act like Him, to talk like Him and to do the things He did. Jesus said:

> **Verily, verily, I say unto you, He that believeth on me, the works that I do shall he do also; and greater**

77

works than these shall he do; *because I go unto my* *Father.*

(John 14:12, italics mine)

Most people do not believe that, so how can they be like Jesus when they do not believe in doing the works that Jesus did, much less greater works?

Be Anchored *and* Built Up

But there is more than walking in Jesus, Paul said. He wrote to the Colossian Christians that they should be rooted in Jesus *and* built up in Him, as they had been taught. Walk like Jesus, be rooted in Him, and then be built up (matured) in Him.

Rooted and built up in him, and stablished in the **faith, as ye have been taught, abounding therein with** **thanksgiving.**

(Verse 7)

The word *rooted* is very interesting. In the Greek, it literally means "to become stable,"[8] so that you are not moving around. Many Christians are transients. They flip-flop around like birds flittering from tree to tree and bush to bush. They are in one church this Sunday and another the next Sunday.

As a Christian, you need to settle down and put roots down somewhere. Surely there is a church somewhere in your vicinity that meets your needs. Of course, the best way is to go where the Holy Spirit

---

[8]New Strong's Concordance, 4492, p. 63.

gives you a witness and to stay there until He moves you, whether or not your soul likes the church, the pastor or the people.

Being *built up in Him* gives the impression of continuous action. For example, you can construct a house in such a way that it can be added to. With the right plans, you could keep building and keep building. That is the sense of *being built up in Him.*

Three things Paul wanted them to remember: *to be rooted, built up and established.* I am established by faith on the basis of the Word of God. That is what *roots* me in Christ. Consequently, when the winds of adversity blow, I remain steady. I am not moved by what I see, I am only moved by what I believe.

The apostle pointed out to them that *they had been taught* and they should *abound* in their teaching with thanksgiving. I was a Christian for a long time before I was taught anything. Sunday services were emotional theatrics, or they were platforms for the preacher's eloquence. His messages were spoken beautifully, but there was no life in them.

You did not learn anything, but you would go away saying, "That was a wonderful messsage! Pastor was at his best today. I have never heard him do better."

But if you honestly and sincerely began to think about what the message was, or if someone asked you what it was about, you would think, "Well, what did he really say?"

Most of the time, there was nothing in the messages to take away and use to change your life. Church went on like that week after week, and I was starving to death spiritually. I could not understand what the problem was. I had a desire and a zeal for God, but it was not being directed or fulfilled.

Personally, I believe preaching is for sinners and teaching is for believers. Preaching sounds good, and people like to hear something inspiring. But God has given me, and every other Christian, the tools to be self-motivated. We should not have to sit around and wait for something to be said to motivate or inspire us.

However, if we want to move out and do the work of the ministry, we *have* to be taught. I needed teaching. I needed knowledge that would keep the economic wolf away from the door. The world economic system is designed to choke you, to keep you in a trap. Food prices go up, clothes go up, utilities go up and gasoline certainly has gone up.

The Body of Christ needs to be taught how to walk in Christ, how to be rooted and grounded in Him and how to be established and anchored in Him.

6

The Ways of Man vs.
the Ways of God
(Col. 2:8-14)

Beware lest any man spoil you through philosophy and vain deceit, after the tradition of men, after the rudiments of the world, and not after Christ.
(Col. 2:8)

In this verse, two principles are placed in juxtaposition to each other: One is the ways of man, and the other is the ways of God.

Believers have a great responsibility to discern between the ways of man and the ways of God. Sometimes people have a difficult time making that separation, because there are many things in the ways of man that basically are good or positive.

Sometimes people get caught up in doing positive or "good" things, and think they are following the ways of God. Then they find out that actually they have been following the traditions of men by doing some "good" things that do not produce life.

The things they are doing may produce some temporary relief, but they do not bring any help for the future. Feeding the hungry and clothing the poor are "good," but does that help feed them next week, next month or next year? Giving something to meet immediate needs is sometimes like putting bandages on a cancer.

Why is that person hungry? *Why* is that person naked? Bandages keep sores from being infected by dirt and dust, and so forth. But they do not bring healing to the problem, and man's "good" works are nothing but bandages on the circumstances. Only taking Christ to those in want is what will truly bring the answers they need in order for their circumstances to change.

Traditions of men are "vain deceits." There are some churches where the ushers will put you out if you try to participate in communion without being a member of their church or denomination. Some people who watch my television program get upset if I sit on the edge of the communion table. *"That table is holy,"* they write to me. No, it is not. That table is only a piece of wood. There is nothing intrinsically holy about the table itself. It only becomes holy when it is being used during the commuion time when the holy elements representing Jesus' body and blood are on it. At that time, I do not sit on the table.

Many Christians have been pulled into "vain deceits" through churches that tell them they cannot do this and cannot do that. Usually, they never read the Bible to find out whether what they are being told is true or not.

Another "religious" tradition that some people are sensitive about has to do with musical instruments in the church. There are some churches where you dare not have drums, a piano or an organ inside the church building. They feel that such instruments are sacrilegious. Musical instruments are spoken of in the Bible. I do not understand why people have such a problem with them, but for some churches it is traditional not to have music in the church.

People become blinded by their traditions, and you cannot discuss these things peaceably with them — in fact, sometimes, they even become irrational. You can show them what the Bible says, and they will just look at it and say, "Well, we do not teach it like that in our church." Not even God can help them. The only person who can help them is them, and if they are not willing to be helped, *there is nothing anyone can do about it!*

In other ministries, women cannot wear pants — not even pants that are *made* for women. Members of those churches will even go so far as to say that a woman is not saved if she wears pants!

That is the reason traditions are "vain deceits"; they often lead Christians off on tangents that are unimportant to their spiritual life or even could destroy them.

> **For in him dwelleth *all* the fulness of the Godhead bodily.**
>
> **(Col. 2:9, italics mine)**

The Godhead is the Father, Son and the Holy Spirit. That means whatever the Father is, and whatever the Holy Spirit is, also is manifested in the Son. God is a Spirit (John 4:24), and we must worship

Him in spirit and in truth. That means we worship God with our real selves and with the Word, because His Word *is* truth.

For us to be able to do this, we must have faith. You cannot worship God, a Spirit who is invisible to you, without *faith*. You must worship Him by faith and not by sight.

The Godhead is Within You

Another aspect of verse 9 is that if Christ is in you, so is the Godhead. What a potential resource to draw from! The Church as a corporate entity has never seen this, only certain individuals from time to time and from generation to generation. The average Christian has never realized this truth; otherwise, nothing would be impossible to him.

But this truth is not deliberately *hidden* from believers. Anyone who will truly believe the Word can see it. There is no mystical, special "code" or "key" you must have to see "deeper truths."

If the Godhead is in you, why are you whipped and defeated, scared and afraid? Why do Christians have inferiority complexes, with the Godhead within them? The reason is that most Christians do not take this verse and others like it seriously. When they hear or read these truths, they seem like so many words or religious jargon to most people.

Verse 10 says we are complete in Jesus, who is the head of all principality and power (rule and authority). *Complete* means "totally, entirely full," with nothing left out. How many Christians really believe that? I doubt that very many do.

One lady heard me say something like this, and she thought, "You know what? I *can* do something about my weight. I can do all things through Christ. I can regulate my weight."

At that time, she was a size 14. Now, she is a size 10, and she is maintaining that size. She likes to eat, and she can cook. She can cook food that would make you fifteen sizes too big! But now, she can control her appetite and her weight, because she received a revelation of Christ within her. She likes the size she is now — and so does her husband!

I refuse to let anything outside of the Word of God have authority over me. Weight is one of the areas in which I had problems. My wife, Betty, and I are always on a diet (not diet food, we hate it!) — a spiritual diet. We believe we can do all things though Christ who strengthens us (Phil. 4:13), and our weight now stays where it ought to be.

I am not talking about anything "flaky" or presumptuous, such as casting calories out of food! We regulate our appetites, the amount of food we eat and we discipline our bodies. Also, we exercise.

The Bible was written for the direction and instruction of believers. You cannot begin to understand it until you are born again. And many Christians do not yet understand that being born again makes them *brand-new people*.

Since God is a Spirit, and we are spirits living in physical bodies, much of the Bible is written about things having to do with the spirit or the soul. Less is written concerning the physical body. However, there are principles, instructions and examples given for all three areas.

When I was born again, I did not understand that something happened only on the inside of me. I thought people meant something happened to the body also. After a few months, when the habits of the flesh began to come back, I thought perhaps I had not really gotten saved. And I know many other Christians have the same lack of understanding.

But the body did not change, as I explained in a previous chapter of this book. When I say *you*, I am not talking to your body. I am talking to the person on the inside who has been recreated, made a new creature in Christ Jesus. Your body is simply a house in which you live and look out the windows (eyes), or a suit of clothes made of flesh and blood.

You must take control of that house, however, or it will go "hog wild." Your "suit of clothes" will run you and not you it, if you are not disciplined. Your body does not know the difference between saved and unsaved, holy and unholy. It will do whatever you let it do.

The life of God is within you; therefore, you *can* rule over your soul and body.

Paul tried to explain this to the Colossian Christians.

Circumcision Without Hands

In verse 11, Paul wrote about a kind of circumcision and about putting off the sins of the flesh.

In whom also ye are circumcised with the circumcision made without hands, in putting off the body of the sins of the flesh by the circumcision of Christ.

Circumcision was something Jewish believers had tried to impose on the Gentiles. The controversy over whether born-again believers in Christ needed to be circumcised in the natural continued for several years after the Day of Pentecost, all across the early Church.

By the time of Christ, the Jewish people had come to believe that circumcision was not just a sign of being part of the Abrahamic covenant, but it was necessary for "salvation." Greeks and Romans did not practice circumcision, so under the Roman Empire, the Jews had become known as "the circumcision" (Acts 10:45), and Gentiles as "the uncircumcision."

The rite God instituted with Abraham had become a symbol of being a chosen people. In fact, Jews had stopped thinking of it in connection with Abraham's covenant and had begun to connect it only with the Mosaic Law (John 7:22, Acts 15:1). Therefore, this ritual had become a matter of racial pride (Phil. 3:4-6).

Finally, the matter was settled when James, the brother of Jesus, who was considered head of the church at Jerusalem, and other elders ruled that Gentiles were not to be subjected to the "law" as represented in the Judaism of Jesus' day. Circumcision was not to be imposed on those under the New Covenant (Acts 15:13-29).

Because he wrote, *"circumcision made without hands"* (Col. 2:11), we know Paul was not talking about a physical operation, but a spiritual one. He wanted the Colossians to have a true understanding of what circumcision really meant. We do know, however, that since a physical circumcision has to do with cutting away something, spiritual circumcision must also involve a cutting-away process.

The words *"body of the sins of the flesh"* (v. 11) mean "body of the sinful nature." There is a sin nature in man that manifests itself in sinful actions. But the nature must have a body to work through, just as gas and oil must have pipes to flow through in order for them to manifest in homes, businesses and other places.

So the physical body becomes the instrument the sinful nature works through, and each of us has the responsibility to do something about it. As far as God is concerned, the sinful nature has been rendered inoperative, but it is up to us to see the new nature (instead of the old one) manifested outwardly.

What happens with spiritual circumcision is this: Just as a surgeon takes a knife to cut away the foreskin of the male, so God takes the knife of His power and, in love, cuts away the "foreskin" of the authority of the sinful nature from around the human spirit. He sees that it is gone. However, most Christians never deal with the habits of soul and body that cause them to live as old creatures, while all of the time they have been created new.

In Romans 6:6, Paul expounds on this truth.

Knowing this, that our old man is crucified with him, that the body of sin might be destroyed, that henceforth we should not serve sin.

Your natural body has not been destroyed, has it? So we know that what was crucified with Christ was not the literal physical body. The fact that Paul said, from the time the old nature is crucified with Christ, we *should not* sin means that we *could* sin. If sinning were no longer possible, he would have said, "You will no longer sin." Instead, he wrote, "You *should* no longer sin."

A better translation of verse 6 would be: *"Knowing this, that our old man is crucified with Him, that our body of the sinful nature might be rendered inactive, that henceforth we should not serve sin."*

So, as a Christian, if you are walking in sin, you cannot blame God or the devil. You have no one to blame but yourself. You have the opportunity to be the pilot of your own aircraft, the captain of your own faith. Not even your wife or husband, or parents, can make the choice not to sin for you.

When I was younger, there were times when I walked the streets of Los Angeles trying to get a job. I would see people not as well qualified as I get jobs because they were white and I was black. I would see children come to school in chauffeur-driven Cadillacs.

And I would say, "Why was I not born white? Why was I not born rich?"

Other times I would say, "I wish I had not done that. I wish I could start over and do things differently. I wish my parents had stayed behind me and made me get the right grades in school, instead of letting me just pass the time there in order to graduate."

Friend, if you ever said those or similar things, now is your chance to start over. God, through Christ, gives you a chance to make a new start. After you are born again, you cannot blame the white man or the black man or the red man or the yellow man or the green man! You cannot blame being poor or having no education for what happens to you.

You *are* a new creature. God is your source, but He has given you the ability and all of the necessary ingredients to succeed. With the Godhead within, you can do anything God says you can do in His Word. But He will not do it *for* you. The choices are yours.

Just having the ability provided to you does not guarantee success. It is *you* that makes the difference. Paul was saying that the body of the sinful nature has been rendered inactive. It has no right to lord it over you anymore — but it will if you let it!

You may ask, "What am I supposed to do about it?

Count Yourself Dead to Sin

Likewise reckon ye also yourselves to be dead indeed unto sin, but alive unto God through Jesus Christ our Lord.

(Rom. 6:11)

He meant that we must treat our bodies as if they were dead, because they have been rendered dead to sin — but this is meant in a spiritual, not literal, sense. If I do not treat my body as if it were dead, it will go and do what it used to do — and more!

That is where the problem lies in the Christian life. This new life does not automatically work. If your body has cravings, it does not mean you are not saved. It does not mean you are not spiritual, nor does it mean you do not love God. Your body has not been born again. If it is changed, it will be changed through you making the right choices and taking authority over it.

Again, this is why faith is so important, and why I teach on faith all of the time. You get saved by faith, and you count your body dead by faith. Paul said in Romans 6:12 not to let sin reign or rule in the body so that you would obey what the body wants to do.

That must mean the body wants to rule. But you do not have to let it, and there is no vacation from ruling over the body. You have to work on it all of the time. Satan would like you to relax and take time off from keeping the body under control.

The devil knows the old nature of mankind very well. He knows that if he applies pressure long enough, most people will say, "What is the use?" They will want to throw in the towel and give up.

Neither yield ye your members as instruments of unrighteousness unto sin: but yield yourselves unto God, as those that are alive from the dead, and your members as instruments of righteousness unto God. For sin shall not have dominion over you: for ye are not under the law, but under grace.

(Rom. 6:13,14)

The sinful nature will not have dominion over you, provided you *count your body dead* (v. 11). This whole concept is so important to the Christian life, and I want to make it as plain as I can. The area of controlling the body is where many Christians miss out on the victorious life.

We talked in an earlier chapter about "presenting your body as a living sacrifice" (Rom. 12:1). Why do you need to do that? *You* are responsible for presenting it, offering the body up to Christ, as a living sacrifice.

Under the Old Covenant, everything that was offered up as a sacrifice was something that was already dead. However, under the New Covenant, God says to offer a "living sacrifice," not a dead one.

Jesus has already redeemed us, once and for all! We are to offer our bodies as an act of faith and as our part of conforming to the image of Christ outwardly.

Your body is Satan's battleground, and so is your mind. Whether you yield to the world's temptations, under Satan's influence, or to yourself as a spirit under the Holy Spirit's influence, is entirely up to you. Whichever one you yield to is the one who will have dominion in your life.

If you take authority over your body and yield your will to the Spirit of God, then you will do things that are consistent with the Word of God. That will cause you to rise above the circumstances and be the master instead of the victim. If you allow your body to rule you, it will drag you down into an early grave.

Get your body in line with the Word, then you can live in the rarefied atmosphere of God's very best.

You do not have to live on the bottom end of the spiritual spectrum. You can live above and not beneath, but you are the one who has to do it. The good news is that through Christ in you, you can do it!

In Colossians 2:12, Paul wrote the rest of what happens after spiritual circumcision:

> **Buried with him in baptism, wherein also ye are risen with him through the faith of the operation of God, who hath raised him from the dead.**
> **(See also Rom. 6:4 and Acts 2:24).**

Water baptism is the symbol of the death, burial and Resurrection of Jesus. When we accept Jesus as our Savior, we become identified with Christ in His death, burial and Resurrection. Symbolically, we are following Jesus. The old spirit-man died and was reborn as a new creature in Christ Jesus. If a man dies, you bury him. Therefore, water baptism is the symbolic burial of the old and the symbolic resurrection of the new.

> **And you, being dead in your sins and the uncircumcision of your flesh, hath he quickened together with him, having forgiven you all trespasses; Blotting out the handwriting of ordinances that was against us, which was contrary to us, and took it out of the way, nailing it to his cross.**
> **(Col. 2:13,14)**

In verse 13, the word *all* refers to everything in the past. When God sees you raised with Jesus from the dead, He does not see anything you did or anything you were before that time. The moment you accept Christ as your Savior, everything sinful in your past becomes as though it never existed.

The world says, ''I am forgiving what you have done, but I am never going to forget it.''

God says, ''As far as I am concerned, what you did never happened.''

The words *''blotting out''* mean ''to erase.'' What happens when something is erased? You cannot see where it has been, if you have a good eraser. And God has the only eraser of sins in the universe — the blood of Jesus.

''Ordinance'' means a law, a statute or a regulation. Those ordinances were against us. The Law of Moses was ''against'' Israel, because the Israelites were not able to keep it. All the Law did was to let people know what sin was. All it was designed for was to point sin out, to let sin be counted as sin.

From Adam to Moses, sin was in the world. However, sin is not counted against you when there is no law. If there is no law that says, ''Thou shalt not steal,'' then you could not sin against it by stealing, could you? A law must be established in order for there to be a lawbreaker. If there is no speed limit, you could not be arrested, no matter how fast you drove.

The Law was given by God in order to *expose* sin, to bring it into the open and make wrongdoing clear to mankind. Sin has no strength apart from the Law (1 Cor. 15:56). Before faith came, Paul said, man was kept under the Law and shut up to the faith that should afterwards be revealed (Gal. 3:23).

However, simply because believers since Christ are not *under* the Law of Moses does not mean we are "lawless." We have a higher law and a better covenant. That means where much is given, much is required (Luke 12:48). *More* is required of us than was required of the Old Covenant believers.

They were not to murder; we are not even to hate.

They were not to commit adultery; we are not even to let our minds think lustful thoughts.

The New Covenant operates by love, not by law.

7

Jesus Brought Life, Not Religion
(Col. 2:15-23)

Paul started this letter by expressing how grateful he was for the Colossians and their faith in Christ.

Then he prayed for them to grow in spiritual maturity. He let them know he was praying for them to walk worthy of Christ, to be fruitful in good works and to be strengthened with patience and longsuffering.

The third thing he wrote, which I discussed in chapters 1-6, was an explanation of Christ's total sufficiency for believers.

Jesus is not only Savior, He is Lord of every power and authority, the Reconciler of all things to God and the Source of new life to Christians. He embodies the entire Godhead, and makes every born-again person complete in Him.

In Colossians 2:15, Paul started to explain another aspect of Christ's victory on the cross — His conquering of all heavenly powers. Why worship angels, when both God's angels and fallen angels are now subject to Jesus?

When Paul said Jesus *spoiled principalities and powers*, he was referring to the demon hosts of Satan.

He used the same terminology in Ephesians 6:12, where he added *"rulers of the darkness of this world and spiritual wickedness in high places."*

Spoiling Principalities and Powers

Satanic forces are divided into four basic ranks, ranging from a lower to a higher degree of responsibility. "Principalities" are the lowest rank, then comes the "powers." Next are the "rulers of the darkness of this world," and finally, "the spiritual wickedness in high [heavenly] places."

The word *spoil* is unfamiliar to us today, when used in this context. Years ago, in the military, if a high-ranking officer did something that was a disgrace to his regiment, he lost his rank and his position. The regimental commander would assemble all of the personnel in whatever camp or place they were. Then, he would not only denounce the man in front of them, but rip off of his uniform any buttons, medals or whatever else showed his rank or position.

What this verse in Colossians means is that Jesus took all of Satan's lieutenants and stood them up in front of the entire universe and stripped them naked. They had nothing to hide behind and nowhere to go.

Jesus stripped them of all authority and triumphed over them. He does not have to defeat Satan and his hordes; He has already done it!

Now is the judgment of this world: now shall the prince of this world be cast out. And I, if I be lifted up from the earth, will draw all men unto me.
(John 12:31,32)

Because Jesus had already spoiled Satan's domain and "made a show" of fallen angels and demons, the religious rituals of the Old Covenant, including circumcision, were no longer necessary or effective. Colossians were not to let anyone "judge" them in matters of rituals, fasting, keeping certain church holidays and so forth.

In other words, *no more legalism* and *no more Pharisaism* — no more "religion."

There were believers among the Jews who tried to accept the new birth while keeping the religion of Judaism with all of its legalistic prohibitions and commandments.

New believers were not to be commanded to keep all of the feast days, nor to keep the Jewish rules that covered cooking and what foods could or could not be eaten.

> **Let no man therefore judge you in meat, or in drink, or in respect of an holy day, or of the new moon, or of the sabbath days.**
>
> **(Col. 2:16)**

As I said earlier about religion, it will put you in bondage and bring confusion. Jesus did not say He came that we might have religion. He said, "I came that you might have true life, that you might be raised from spiritual death, and that you might have both spiritual and natural life more abundantly" (John 10:10, paraphrased).

Religion Adds and Takes Away

Society in those days was not as it is today, where we have many atheists, agnostics and strange doctrines. Today, we have several systems of thought and politics that are founded on a lack of belief in God and in the Bible as His true Word and in its direction for men's lives.

However, in Paul's day — in fact, for thousands of years previously — practically everyone was involved in a religion of some kind.

Some cultures worshiped the creature instead of the Creator (Rom. 1:25), which meant they worshiped trees, the sun, moon, and stars and so forth. Others actually worshiped demons in the form of statues and images, and practiced polytheism — a religion of many gods. Only a handful of philosophers in the few hundred years before Christ had dared not to believe in some type of a god at all.

Even the relationship with Almighty God that the line of Seth down to Jesus had enjoyed became "religion" to most of the Jews by the time of Jesus' ministry. What we call "Judaism" really began when the Jews were cut off from the Promised Land and from temple worship during their seventy-year exile in Babylon.

At that time, many commentaries began to be written and added to what we call Old Testament writings. During that time, and also during the growth of the sect of the Pharisees (about 200 years before Christ), rituals were added and men's doctrines and traditions were added to the writings of Moses and the prophets.

Jesus spent a large portion of His ministry showing the religious leaders of His time the difference between their religious beliefs and what the Old Testament writings really said. But, in the end, most of them chose religion instead of life. Even some of those who chose the New Covenant were reluctant to let go of their religion.

Paul, in several of his epistles to various churches, fought this mixture as hard as he could.

If their religion had been sufficient for salvation and had it been made up of truth, Jesus would not have taught against parts of it. As it was, He fought it and religion crucified Him. Religious leaders tried to discredit Him from the beginning of His ministry.

Religion is man's attempt, by his own thinking and his own interpretations, to reach God. It is an attempt to "bring God down" to man's level of understanding. A relationship with God takes you up to the level of Jesus, who literally came down to earth to seek the lost and redeem them.

Religion is man's attempt to make himself acceptable to God. Religion always ends up with an emphasis on works, on somehow earning God's love and approval. Because man can never earn what God gave us as a free gift, religion is "trying to climb up into the Kingdom some other way" (John 10:1, paraphrased), and it ends up bringing bondage.

Paul said that rules, regulations, setting of certain days to fast and so forth, were but *"a shadow of things to come; but the body is of Christ"* (v. 17).

Body in this verse is a little misleading in the King James Version. Paul is using it in the sense of "substance" or "reality," just as we might say, "The pictures give you an idea of the subject, but the *body* (substance, reality) of the teaching is in the writing.''

In other words, he said, ''Religious rituals were a shadow of things to come, but the substance or reality is Christ.''

Religion adds to and takes away from the truth about the Godhead, mankind and creation.

Let No Man. . . .

Notice again, that verse 8 says, *''Beware lest any man. . .,''* and verse 16 says, *''Let no man. . .,''* and now verse 18 says again, *''Let no man.''* Three times Paul said, *''Let no man. . . .''* That means a man cannot tell you to do something unless you let him, which means you can keep a man from meddling with you about the things of God.

Beware of Losing Your Reward

> **Let no man beguile you of your reward in a voluntary humility and worshipping of angels, intruding into those things which he hath not seen, vainly puffed up by his fleshly mind, And not holding the Head, from which all the body by joints and bands having nourishment ministered, and knit together, increaseth with the increase of God.**
> **(Col. 2:18,19)**

The word ''beguile'' literally means ''to decide against you or to judge you.''

Paul says let no man *beguile* you, or do not let anyone decide against you or judge you concerning the reward that you will receive from looking to Jesus as your Source and Reality.

Then he ties it in by saying, *". . . your reward in a voluntary humility and worshipping of angels."* The substance of this verse in the Greek is the idea that these false teachers were saying to people, "Look, do you really want to get into worshiping the Lord? Do you want to get close to God? Let me tell you how to do it. The best way to get to God is to worship the angels. That is the first step in getting to God."

That was the philosophy they were bringing to the early Christians. These philosophers were telling people, "You do not have any reward if you are not worshiping angels." *That is vain philosophy!* In fact, that is satanic deception, but that is exactly what those people were doing. They were worshiping angels, and there are still people who worship angels today.

The same wicked spirit who sponsored that philosophy back then is still working in the earth-realm today. There are people who are worshiping this, that and the other, instead of God. And it is vain philosophy.

> **Let no man beguile you of your reward in a voluntary humility and worshipping of angels, intruding into those things which he hath not seen, vainly puffed up by his fleshly mind.**

Being *"vainly puffed up by the fleshly mind"* means getting into pride because you think you know something the average believer does not know. The *fleshly mind* is the sinful nature of the soul and body.

In Second Corinthians 5:17, Paul said any man who receives Christ is a new creature, old things are passed away and all things have become new. However, *all things* cannot mean the body, or you would already have a brand-new, transfigured body. He cannot have been talking about the flesh.

If you were bald when you got saved, you will be bald after you are saved. If you were overweight when you got saved, you will be overweight after you are saved. If you had false teeth or an artificial leg when you got saved, you will still have those things, unless you believe God for a miracle.

So what *old things* passed away? Paul was talking about the old things of the spirit, things that separated us from God: alienation, separation, sin consciousness and spiritual death. All of those things passed away, and now we have spiritual life, a relationship with God and an eternal future with Him. There is fellowship with our heavenly Father, and no condemnation or guilt.

Religion gets its strength from the carnal or fleshly mind that tries to figure things out according to man's own understanding. The minds of men, influenced by demons, are what has gotten the world into the mess we see today. Educated, academic brains making ''logical'' plans and developing ''rational'' systems have brought about the consequences the world is now facing.

The money systems almost have the nations of the world bankrupt. The Federal Reserve System, which is not ''federal'' at all, but a coalition of private banks, practically owns the United States government through loans and the interest on loans.

If you keep listening to the news, particularly about the Middle East, it will scare you! I do not listen to many of the news reports in detail, just the weather and a brief report on world news to keep up with what is going on. All you hear on the national media usually is *bad* news. Listening to a lot of the current news reports can make you become depressed.

In spite of the mess we see and the awful things we hear, there *are* some good things happening. It would be great if the media would tell us how many safe airline flights there were this year, how many people did not rob banks or how many women were not raped, and how many husbands did not beat their wives.

Even with the increasing crime rate, there are more good people than bad, more good things happening than bad, more encouraging events occurring than discouraging ones. What about a "good-news" newspaper? One that would tell us how many people did not die of cancer this week, or how many people did not drown or were not killed in automobile accidents.

The Body Must Depend on the Head

If a person's head were separated from his body, what would happen? That person would have some serious problems! Yet, that has been one of the dangers the Church has faced from the beginning.

Paul was telling the Colossians not to allow anything — false teachings, religious doctrines, worldly thinking and pleasures — to keep them from holding onto the Head. Without the Head, who is Christ, there would be no nourishment and no growth for the Body.

You can get by with only one arm or one leg, but not without your head. If the Church allows anyone or anything to separate us from Christ, it is the same as your body being separated from your head. The result will be death.

The next verses read:

> **Wherefore if ye be dead with Christ from the rudiments of the world, why, as though living in the world, are ye subject to ordinances, (Touch not; taste not; handle not; Which all are to perish with the using;) after the commandments and doctrines of men?**
>
> **(Col. 2:20-23)**

"Wherefore if ye be dead" should actually be rendered, according to the Greek, as: *"Since ye are dead."* That makes quite a difference.

Paul was asking, "Why are you paying attention to the wisdom of the world, to the 'do's' and 'don'ts' of religion when you are not subject to the world anymore? Don't you know all these things will perish? They are temporary, like the commandments and doctrines of men."

In essence, Paul told them, "All of those things perish with the using, just like the food you eat. If you know that you were crucified with Christ, why are you hanging onto all these dead things?"

God does not see us the way we see ourselves. He sees us identified with Christ. When Jesus died, we died. Just as all mankind was in Adam, the first man, when he sinned and was separated from God, all born-again people are now in Jesus when He was raised from the dead (1 Cor. 15:45).

We are the Body of Christ, so we must be as much Christ as the Head. That is the way God sees us, and that is the way we have to see ourselves. Also, using the same analogy, the head makes the decisions and gives directions, and the body is simply to follow the leading of the head. The body does not "think" for itself.

If you ever learn to see yourself as God sees you, it will take you out of the realm of the ordinary and into a supernatural world view. When you realize that, as a born-again child of God, you literally are made in His image, it will not give you a "superiority" complex. But rather all complexes will be removed when you see yourself as a true child of the King.

A Show of Wisdom

"These things you have been getting into," Paul said, "may look like wisdom or like concepts inspired of wisdom, but they are not."

There is another passage of Scripture that will help us understand better what Paul is saying in verse 23, and that is John 1:12,13:

> **But as many as received him, to them gave he power to become the sons of God, even to them that believe on his name; Which were born, not of blood,**

107

nor of the will of the flesh, nor of the will of man, but of God.

Paul said that salvation is not a product of human imagination nor of the human will. You cannot become a child of God by "willing" it, nor even by desiring it, only by *receiving* Christ.

Salvation is not by the will of man! No one can will himself into the good graces of God Almighty. Before my children were born, I believed God for their salvation. However, I could not accomplish their salvation by my *will*, no matter how much I might have wanted to.

They are bone of my bone and flesh of my flesh, but they had to receive Jesus for themselves. I would love to be able to *will* for them to be healthy all the days of their lives, but I cannot. As much as I love my children, I cannot *will* for their well-being.

A better way to describe *will-worship* might be "worship determined out of one's own head, a show of wisdom prescribed by oneself." Man has always mentally devised some way to explain God or to worship God. All those people following religions were sincere — but they were wrong. If anything you are doing is not being done God's way, it is wrong.

People do not even think about having to follow certain procedures to get jobs, or to become American citizens, to open bank accounts, or to file income tax reports. You would not even consider trying to figure out some way to do it *your* way, even if your way were better. Why? You would not waste your time and energy, because you know *your* way would not be accepted.

Why does man think he can figure out a better way of doing things than God already has set down? Why does man think God will accept any way other than that already laid out in the Word? Mankind is deceived by Satan and puffed up in his own wisdom, the fleshly mind (Col. 2:18).

In verse 23, the phrase *"neglecting the body"* really means "hard treatment of the body." In past centuries, and in some remote places even today, some have fallen into this deceit.

Self-flagellation, or whipping one's self, is considered a means of bringing the body under control, or subduing the appetites.

Verse 23 really says: "Those things have a show of wisdom in worship prescribed by oneself, and voluntary hard treatment of the body is not of any value to remedy the indulgences of the flesh."

Eating this thing and not eating that thing will not control the flesh with its desires. All the doctrines that tell you not to eat this, and not to do that, not to go there, and not to wear this and that, or not to cut your hair a certain way are of no value in correcting what is in the flesh.

What is in the flesh is sin, and the only thing that can deal with that is the blood of the Lord Jesus Christ. If you try to *will* sin out of your mind, all you do is deceive yourself. In the end, you will be right back where you started — nowhere!

8
Seek Those Things Which Are Above
(Col. 3:1-8)

With the first verse of chapter three, you can climb to the highest heights of spirituality. If you truly realize what that verse says, you will never get yourself into any kind of trouble. You will never be victimized by your environment or by mental and emotional problems. And, you will be a victor in every area of life, if you will do what verse 2 says.

> **If ye then be risen with Christ, seek those things which are above, where Christ sitteth on the right hand of God. Set your affection on things above, not on things on the earth.**
>
> **(Col. 3:1,2)**

Here again is the idea of identification with Christ, *if you then be risen* with Him. When Jesus rose from the dead, what did that mean concerning His past life? What was involved in His past life was now left behind.

There had been false accusations. Religious leaders called Him a ''winebibber'' (Luke 7:34) and said He was in league with Satan (Luke 11:15). During His three-year ministry, there was increasing persecution and misunderstanding.

But when He rose from the dead, He was a victor over those things. He had conquered the circumstances that had tried to assail Him during His earthly ministry. The Word says that since you are risen with Christ, God sees you as being triumphant over all the things of *your* past life.

God sees you on top of frustration, on top of temptation, on top of persecution, on top of sickness and disease and on top of hatred and prejudice. He sees you overcoming everything that would hinder you and attempt to keep you in bondage.

However, most Christians do not believe this, even if they hear it preached and read it in the Word. Even Spirit-filled, Bible-carrying, cassette-playing Christians do not act as if they believe Jesus put them on top. They do what their minds tell them to do and not what the Word of God says.

Paul said that *"since you are risen with Christ,"* seek those things which are above. Instead of that, you are seeking the things your body wants and the things your soul wants. If many Christians do not get what they want, they throw tantrums. They deny faith and say, "That stuff just doesn't work!"

These verses are the same as the words of Jesus in Matthew 6:33:

> **But seek ye first the kingdom of God, and his righteousness; and all these things shall be added unto you.**

The Holy Spirit inspired the writers of the New Testament to include these things to help us avoid the pitfalls of life that the devil has put in our paths in order to trap us.

If the highway department has put up warning signs to prevent accidents, we pay attention. When we see signs saying, "Slow down, danger ahead," we begin to drive at a slower rate of speed. A sign that says, "Bridge Out," moves us to look for another road, another way to get to our destination.

If we see those signs and decide to go on anyhow, would we blame the highway department for the consequences? Christians need to learn to follow the Bible at least as much as they follow signs and warning signals in the world.

Setting the Right Priorities

When I was a child, we used to play a game called "hide-and-go-seek." One person was tagged as "it," and that one would stand at "home base," hiding his or her eyes. Then, after counting up to a certain number, that person would try to find everyone else. All of the rest of us had scattered to hide in places where we thought we would not be found. "It" would then go out to *seek* us.

Paul was telling us to be "it" Christians. We are to *seek* the Kingdom of God, which is not hiding at all. However, "it" is not in the world nor is it in religious places. You find "it" through Jesus and in the Spirit. Most Christians do not believe that if they find God's ways first, all the other things they need will fall into place. Most Christians seek the things of the world and not the things of the spiritual realm.

I hear some single Christians say, "I just don't know why I can't find a mate!"

I know why. It is because they are looking for one, instead of seeking God and letting Him send them a mate. If you have not sought the Lord's help in selecting a spouse, you do not know what you are getting when you find one. All you are seeing is the outside.

Your first priority *must* be seeking God's Kingdom: His Word, His principles and His ways of looking at life and doing things. Verse 2 means what it says — to set our minds on things above.

I have counseled with people who say, "Pastor Price, I'm going out of my mind!"

I am not making fun of them. My heart goes out to them. I am merely making a point by showing you what people say without even thinking about it. Their souls — minds, wills, and emotions — are perhaps going through turmoil, but they are not really losing their minds.

Sometimes I will ask, "Well, where is your mind set? What is it that is bothering you so?"

Usually, they will tell me of an unfulfilled desire. Perhaps, it is a young lady who wants a husband.

She will say, "Well, I want a husband." I respond, "But the Bible tells us to set our minds on things above."

"Am I not supposed to have a husband, then?"

"Well, sure," I answer, "but do you want to play Russian roulette? Or do you want the right husband? Do you want to go through a trial-and-error process? Or do you want to be sure you have the right one?"

When you get yourself in the right place spiritually, then God can bring the right person into your life. "Chafing at the bit" and always being frustrated will cause you to mess up and pick the wrong one. Christians must learn to trust God in every area of their lives. He *is* concerned about our marriages, because He is our Father.

How do you set your mind on things above? How do you set your priorities in order? You do that by setting your mind on the Word and by beginning to do what the Word says, trusting God to bring to pass the desires of your heart.

He *will* bring them to pass, according to His Word. Notice that in verse 2, Paul did not write that you cannot have the things of earth. He simply said not to set your mind on them.

Some people have said to me, "If I don't date, how am I going to know if I want to marry this person or that one?"

My answer has to be, "Even if you do date, you will not know whether this is the right person or not."

Your flesh may pick a certain one, but that is the lust of the body. Your mind or emotions may pick another one, but that could be because that person fits the preconceived pattern in your subconscious mind of a husband or wife. When you are tied to that person, you may find out that some idea out of a romantic novel or movie or one which came from watching mom and dad caused you to pick the wrong spouse.

Only God knows you totally and the other person totally. Only God is the perfect matchmaker.

Betty and I were just kids when we married. We were sincere, and we loved each other. But only the grace of God has made our marriage work. And He could do that for us because the first priority for both of us was *to please God.*

Almost everyone with whom we went to school, and who got married about the same time we did, got divorced — some of them more than once. The only thing we have had going for us, which apparently they have not had, is God.

God wants you to be happy. He cares more about your happiness than any earthly father ever could. It hurts Him when you are not happy. If you are miserable, sick and down and out, the Holy Spirit grieves for you. Anything you want or need in this life is a matter of priorities, a matter of putting things in the proper order of importance. If you follow God's order of priorities, you will be happy.

Jesus Is Our Life

Our lives are supposed to be centered on Jesus. When Jesus said He was the truth, the life and the way (John 14:6), what did He mean? He meant that if you will order your life by His life, you will experience abundant living.

When abundance or prosperity is mentioned, many people only think of material things. But "things" are only part of abundant living. Houses, cars, clothes, furniture and even money together form only one part of abundant living.

I would rather have prosperity of spirit. To have the peace of God that passes all understanding is worth more than fourteen Rolls Royces. I would rather have prosperity in my mind than to have it in the physical world.

Colossians 3, verses 3 and 4, explain this further:

> **For ye are dead, and your life is hid with Christ in God. When Christ, *who is our life*, shall appear, then shall ye also appear with him in glory.**
>
> **(Italics mine)**

Christ is our life (v. 4), if we are "dead" and our lives are hidden in Him, when He appears in glory, so will we.

First Corinthians 15:42-44 says:

> **So also is the resurrection of the dead. It [the body] is sown in corruption; it is raised in incorruption: It is sown in dishonour; it is raised in glory; it is sown in weakness; it is raised in power: It is sown a natural body; it is raised a spiritual body. There is a natural body, and there is a spiritual body.**

The Word is what works. It will bring you joy, peace and everything you could ever desire. But even the Word will not help you if you do not do what it says — and do it God's way. Sometimes you have to do it even when your mind and body are telling you to go another way.

The false doctrines and religious practices which were creeping into the Colossian church would have caused them to deny their lives in Christ and eventually to lose their rewards (Col. 2:18). The Apostle Paul tried every way he could think of to pull the Colossian Christians out of the trap Satan had set for them.

At the same time, all of the truths of God — the admonitions, warnings and knowledge which he wrote to them are applicable to us today. We have the same temptations, the same kinds of religious traps, the same kinds of fleshly yearnings and mental confusions.

Colossians 3:5 is very important in understanding how to live a victorious Christian life. In essence, what Paul wrote in this verse is: Do not let your body control your life anymore.

Kill Ungodly Desires

Mortify therefore your members which are upon the earth; fornication, uncleanness, inordinate affection, evil concupiscence, and coveteousness, which is idolatry.

The word *mortify* is the Greek word *nekroo*, which means "to deaden" or "to subdue."[9] The English word *mortify* is only used twice in the New Testament. The other place is in Paul's letter to the Christians at Rome:

---

[9]Strong's *Greek Dictionary of the New Testament*, p. 49, #3499.

> For if ye live after the flesh, ye shall die: but if ye through the Spirit do *mortify* the deeds of the body, ye shall live.
>
> (Rom. 8:13, italics mine)

In that verse, however, Paul used the Greek word *thanatoo*, which means "to kill" or "become dead, [cause to be] put to death, kill, mortify."[10]

So to the Colossians, Paul was speaking figuratively about "putting to death" your members. Literally, he was saying to *subdue* the parts of your body, to bring them under authority. But to the Romans, he spoke in an even stronger way: "Through the Holy Spirit, *kill* the deeds of the body in order to live longer upon the earth."

Mortifying the body and the deeds of the body is necessary for the welfare of the spirit, the real you, and for your body, the house in which you live on earth.

Paul was saying that if you put to death the member of your body that could cause you to commit fornication, you will not commit fornication. Contrary to some beliefs of the past, however, Paul is not talking about a literal physical operation. He is not talking about becoming eunuchs through castration in order to avoid sinning.

Paul was talking about a spiritual operation, receiving a revelation that the flesh *has been* crucified with Christ, that *you* are not your *flesh*, and that you can choose what your flesh does.

---

[10]Ibid, p. 35, #2289.

When the words *inordinate affection* are used in the Bible, they always have a negative connotation. Paul did not mean "over-expectancy." What he meant was caring too much about someone or something, such as a love that suffocates the other person.

"Inordinate affection" are two words in English that translate as one word in Greek: *pathos*, which means, "to suffer," such as "an affection of the mind, a passionate desire."[11]

Concupiscence means "to desire, to lust (after)," or "lustful desires" about anything.[12] With *evil* connected with the word, it is obvious what Paul is talking about. The Bible tells us to "kill" those evil or unlawful desires. This is where some people get into trouble, by meditating on things that can lead to sin.

Sin begins in the mind. If you keep thinking wrong thoughts about sex, you probably will find yourself involved in wrong sexual relationships.

I have used sex as an example, but the same pattern exists with drinking, drugs or smoking. One of the saddest things I have ever seen is someone consumed by a *thing* or by a *desire*.

The *You* Then; The *You* Now

For which things' sake the wrath of God cometh on the children of disobedience; In the which ye also walked some time, when ye lived in them. But now ye also put off all these; anger, wrath, malice, blasphemy, filthy communication out of your mouth.
(Col. 3:6-8)

---

[11]*Vine's Expository Dictionary*, Vol 1, p. 36, #1.
[12]Strong's, p. 31, #1939.

The implication of *"in the which ye also walked some time"* is that at one time the Colossian Christians walked in the things listed in verse 5, but now that they were children of God, they no longer were a party to those things. The word *"walked"* is past tense.

Paul said, "As a child of God, since you are risen with Christ, you do not live or participate in things of the flesh any longer."

The Apostle Paul was saying there ought to be a difference between "the *you* then" and "the *you* now." If there is no difference between you before and after your "conversion," then perhaps nothing really happened to you.

However, the change is not automatic. You have to do something after you accept Christ. You have to put the parts of your body under the authority of God's Word and not let them run amuck. You cannot do what comes naturally. What "comes naturally" will get you into natural trouble, as well as spiritual difficulty.

Paul told them how to stay out of sin and out of trouble. Now that they had stopped walking in those things, they also had to *put off* some other things. Paul said, *". . . ye also put off all these."* Ye means "you." So the responsibility is on the individual Christian.

The "other" things they had to put off were anger, wrath, malice, blasphemy and filthy speech. This is very important practical teaching on how to live as a Christian. We get the idea sometimes that when you are born again, letting go of these things comes automatically.

"To put off" means "to put it away from you." When I take off my coat, I put it away from me. That means I am in one place and my coat is in another. Suppose my coat represents lust, or inordinate affection, or fornication. *I am the one who has to put it off.* That is the only way it got off me. *I did it!*

When I was first saved, I was a new creature inside, but my soul still had a problem with anger. I had not *put anger away from me.* I had a violent temper. I would do things that were so embarrassing I would be ashamed of what I had done. It is a wonder my high school did not charge me for damages to locker doors. I would get angry and bash in the door. Afterwards, I would be so sorry that I would cry.

Thank God for my wife! The average woman would have left me long ago.

The church to which I belonged did not tell me how to do anything. Members would say, "Let go," or "Hold on," but they did not tell me what to let go of or what to hold on to. For a long time, I tried to deal with my temper by myself, until I learned what the Word told me to do.

There may be some instances when a demon is involved in cases of violent tempers, but most of the time what is occurring shows a lack of self-discipline and self-control. You are letting the old nature operate as if you did not even have a new one.

How do you deal with things like this? You simply do what Paul says to do, and take it off.

When I finally learned how to operate by faith, I took off anger. When I really saw what the Holy Spirit had inspired Paul to write to men who, 2,000 years ago, had problems just like mine, I began to deal with my temper.

I used to pray, "O Lord, please take this temper away from me," and I could not understand why God would not do it. Later, I found it was because He had already told *me* to do it.

I said, "Lord, can I really do that? You mean *I* have control over this temper?"

I thought my temper was something I had inherited from my father, because I had heard, "Oh, he's just like his father." But now I had a new Father, one who does not get angry and tear things up.

When I found out that I had the nature of Christ, yet I was letting the outer man go berserk and run amuck, I took control of my body and my soul. I would say, "Stop, in the name of Jesus! You will not embarrass the Father any longer."

After that, when the hound dog next door, the one that once kept me upset by barking at 2:00 A.M., began to bark, I did not get mad.

I would say, "Go on and bark, you dumb dog. You can stay awake, if you want to, but I am going to sleep." And I did!

I found that when I ignored his barking, he would quit. And I began to see something. The devil was using that dog against me, and at first, I had not had sense enough to see it. But when I recognized the barking was being instigated to cause me to lose my temper, I put a stop to that little game of the enemy.

Now, there are times when I purposely raise my voice in a very stern manner in order for people to understand I mean business. But as far as letting my temper control me, I do not walk in that any more. I stopped getting angry. I put off anger. It has been years since I "lost" my temper.

The old me does not live in this body any longer. Praise God!

Let the Lord Handle Things

Another way to make it easy to "put off" these things Paul mentions, and others of the old nature that he did not list, is to let the Lord handle problems and situations. Then anger and other wrong emotions do not rise up.

Wrath is where anger goes a step further and becomes revengeful. The thought, "I'm going to get you. You just wait," is *wrath*. When you move into that kind of thinking, you are treading on dangerous ground.

It is far better to forget something done to you than to hold a grudge. And better yet, to forgive the person completely and let it be as if it never happened. Many times, whatever has been done to you will not hurt you as much as holding a grudge over it will.

Unforgiveness will not hurt the one who injured you nearly as much as it will hurt you. Unforgiveness is "cutting off your nose to spite your own face." Let God take care of it. He is the One who said, *"Vengeance belongeth unto me, I will recompense"* (Heb. 10:30).

People talk about me all of the time. Some even lie about me. There are times when I am tempted as much as you might be to rise up in indignation. Instead, I take hold of the Word and turn the situation over to the Lord.

I have had people come up to me and say, "Pastor Price, I want to ask you to forgive me."

When I ask what for, they say, "Well, I have been saying some things about you that were not too nice."

I tell them they already are forgiven. They have not hurt me. They have only hurt themselves. That is obvious because guilt hurts. Without a hurting conscience, they might not have asked my forgiveness.

In addition, holding on to anger, wrath, malice and unforgiveness can make you sick. Those dark, negative emotions can open the door for the devil to put sickness on you. When people hold on to malice, anger and all that other junk, they are poisoning their own cisterns, contaminating their own fountains.

In some ministries today, there are people who will not speak to other people in the same church. Frankly, I would not waste five seconds holding something against someone. It simply is not worth it!

There are black Christians who hold things against whites, and there are white Christians who hold things against blacks. There are Christians who hold malice against me because I am black — as if anyone in the world can help what race he or she is born into. We have no choice as to what race we are.

Some husbands are holding things against their wives, and vice versa. It does not matter what people have done to you: *Let the Lord handle it!* I guarantee you He will bring you out on top, and the very ones who have tried to harm you will come and ask your forgiveness. I have had it happen time and time again.

"Blasphemy" in verse 8 is "ungodly speech," a way of talking that is not befitting a child of the King. And *"filthy communication"* is telling dirty jokes and using foul language. This should not be heard coming out of the mouths of Christians.

You may say, "Well, I can't help myself," but I say you *can* because God said you could through the Apostle Paul's writings. If you are not in control of your members, then you are in trouble.

God will handle situations and problems in your relationships and in your environment if you turn them over to Him. But He will not do your part of controlling your members for you. That is *your* responsibility!

9
Putting on the New Life
(Col. 3:9-15)

In verses 9-15, Paul wrote about other things we need to put off, and then he provides a list of things we are to put on.

Lie not one to another, seeing that ye have *put off the old man with his deeds.*
(Col. 3:9, italics mine)

There are various ways to lie. There is the *overt* or "deliberate" lie, the "little white lie" told out of a mistaken idea of not hurting someone's feelings, and lies of omission — not telling the whole truth.

For example, a man calls his wife from the office and tells her he is going to be late getting home because some business associates from out of town have arrived to go over some files. He *is* going to be late, but not for the reason he gave. Then he hangs up the phone and spends an hour and a half in a bar meeting "the guys" for a beer.

A newlywed wants to cook a special dinner for her husband, and spends a lot of time preparing the meal. He comes home from work to find candles on the tables, the best silver and china out on the best lace tablecloth. He also finds that her main dish includes garden peas which he hates.

He "lies" by going ahead and eating a lot to please her. His lying to be kind in order not spoil her pleasure will backfire, for unless he sooner or later tells the truth, he will be eating that "special casserole" the rest of his life! If he does not tell her, and she finds out later, the hurt and lack of trust will cause more trouble in their relationship than his telling her the truth in the beginning would have.

How much more will she be hurt five years later? She may begin to wonder what else he has not told her for fear of "hurting her feelings." The devil certainly will not lose the opportunity to whisper, "What else has he been lying to you about?"

You can lie on your income tax returns by not reporting certain income you receive in cash. Kids learn to lie by writing made-up excuses for absences in school. A lie is a lie! There is no such thing as a "little white lie." All of them are lies and they are from the kingdom of darkness.

We have gotten to the point of expecting the world to lie, even if it is by "stretching things." Which of us really believes advertisements anymore? Lying has become a way of life for the world. If you are not careful, you will fall into the same pattern of deceit.

Christians need to develop the habit of *always* telling the truth, because that is what the Word of God says we are to do. Whatever you are, it is because you have *learned* to be that way. People are not born lazy and shiftless, nor are they born liars.

If you are lazy, you have practiced and trained yourself through habit to be that way. Likewise, habitual lying is the result of "training." Everyone who succeeds in life has had to discipline himself. He had to do things he did not want to do, go to meetings he did not want to attend and visit a client when he would rather have played golf.

Christians need to become diligent, to stop being lazy in spiritual matters. Maturing in Christ takes the same commitment and the same kind of dedication that it takes to succeed at anything in the world.

In John 8:31, Jesus said to those Jews who believed in Him, *"If ye continue in my word,* then are ye my disciples indeed."

He did not say, "If you start out in the Word, or rejoice about the Word or shout hallelujah over the Word, you are my disciples."

Jesus said, "If you *continue* in my Word, you truly are my disciples."

Then Jesus told them that they would know the truth, and the truth would make them free (John 8:32). So how am I to be made free? How are you to be made free? The only way is *by continuing in the Word,* not by reading it just on Sundays or holidays. I found that out a long time ago.

The more I continued in the Word, the more the passages and verses became revelation-knowledge to me. They came alive, and I committed myself to dealing in the truth. Sometimes people are offended by it. They would rather for me to "soft pedal," or put a "sugar coating" around the truth to make it more palatable. I cannot do that.

I have studied the four gospels, and I do not find any example in them that shows Jesus dealing with an issue without telling the truth. That was another reason why the religious leaders of His day got upset with Him. He told it like it was, and they did not always like the truth.

As Christians, we need to be honest with each other. Jesus said:

> A new commandment I give unto you, That ye love one another; as I have loved you, that ye also love one another. By this shall all men know that ye are my disciples, if ye have love one to another.
> (John 13:34,35)

Love does not lie. Love always tells the truth. I tell people not to ask me anything or give me anything if they are not prepared to hear the truth. I tell the truth as nicely as I can, but if someone gets hurt feelings, that is not my problem.

Put on the "New Man"

In Colossians 3, verse 10, Paul wrote:

> And have put on the new man, which is renewed in knowledge after the image of him that created him.

Notice that *you* have put off the old man with his deeds (v. 9), now *you* must put *on* the new man. And this "new man" has been renewed in the image of Jesus, who created all things (Col. 1:16). As I said before, neither your body nor your life-style will automatically change when you become a Christian. *You* must change them.

The good news is that while you were the "old man," you could not change many things about yourself. Now that you are a new man, you *can* put on the things that go with someone who is created in the image of Jesus.

When the Bible says "the old man," it means the old life-style, the old way of doing things. Paul indicated that "the old man" meant lying, anger, wrath, malice, blasphemy, filthy conversation and so forth (Col. 3:8,9). You "put them off" by no longer doing them. Then you must start *doing* the things shown in the Word and through the Holy Spirit instead.

"Yeah, but how do I do that?" How do you curse someone out? You open your mouth and words pour out. Only, now, open your mouth and let nice things, good things, friendly things pour out, instead of all that garbage. The "old things" are a matter of habit that must be broken. You will have to work at it. But because you have a commandment from God to do this, you know that you can do it through Jesus.

You cannot do it, however, apart from the knowledge of the Word. You cannot *know* Jesus apart from the Word. You cannot "put off the old man and put on the new" in your own strength. And you may not always feel like doing it. But, remember, feelings do not count. You cannot go by feelings. That is "walking by sight."

Your body and mind will be telling you to do something else. Thoughts will tell you that it is too hard to resist the old habits. But the spirit-man that is the real you will be saying, "No, this is God's way. This is what I have to do to enjoy the fullness of God."

Staying in the Word and then acting upon it is what brings about a quality life-style in Jesus. A victorious life does not just happen.

You may think, "That sounds to me like a whole lot of work." Really, it is not any more work than all of the foolish things, the non-productive things, that you were accustomed to doing. The only reason it seems hard is because you are making a change, and human nature has something in it since the Fall that rebels against change.

It does not matter what the change is — unless it is something so much to a person's benefit that he would be foolish to resist — most of us want to resist change. However, a wise person will readily make whatever changes are necessary.

Only a fool keeps moving doggedly in the wrong direction. Wisdom dictates that there are always times when one needs to make a change.

Have you ever noticed how easy it is to curse? All those words I used more than forty years ago, I could let come out of my mouth again. I have not forgotten them. But once you reeducate yourself to speak God's words and to do things God's way, spiritual things become easier, and you now have the Holy Spirit to help you.

It will become just as easy to spend time praying as it was not to pray. It will become just as easy to study the Bible as not to study it. What is hard is making up your mind to pray and to stay in the Word. Once your mind is made up, once you are committed, the rest is comparatively easy.

The "new man" is God's man. The new man is a spiritual man. The new man is a man recreated in the image and likeness of God. The new man on the inside, who has been reborn, searches the Word of God to find the perameters of his new life. Then the new man begins to put those things into operation through his mind.

Man is a spirit like God who is a Spirit. Man is not an animal, contrary to many educational and scientific beliefs today. You can believe in evolution if you want to, but I believe the Bible.

> **But God giveth it a body as it hath pleased him, and to every seed his own body. All flesh is not the same flesh: but there is one kind of flesh of men, another flesh of beasts, another of fishes, and another of birds.**
>
> **(1 Cor. 15:38,39)**

If there were not any other verses in the Word to prove that man is a spirit and not of the animal class, the above verses would be enough. All flesh is not the same; man has one flesh, animals another.

So how could animal flesh ever give birth to human flesh? The point is that we are created spirits in the image of God, *the* Spirit Being who created us.

Put on the new man who acts like God.

> **Where there is neither Greek nor Jew, circumcision nor uncircumcision, Barbarian, Scythian, bond nor free: but Christ is all, and in all.**
> **(Col. 3:11)**

"In all" means all those who have allowed Jesus to recreate them through the new birth. Paul did not mean Christ was in everyone in the world. He was writing to Christians only, so when he wrote *"in all,"* he meant only Christians.

His Mercy Endures Forever

We are told in the Word that God's mercy endures forever (Ps. 106:1). The Word also says that we are recreated in God's image. How long does *your* mercy endure? If you are like your Father, should you not have enduring mercy?

> **Put on therefore, as the elect of God, holy and beloved, bowels of mercies, kindness, humbleness of mind, meekness, longsuffering.**
> **(Col. 3:12)**

These are some of the things Christians should be putting on as new men. Mercy is not a quality that is in you, it is an act you perform, a choice you make. You are to be merciful *operationally*, by choice and action. God is merciful *intrinsically*. He *is* mercy.

God is still saving people after 2,000 years. His mercy endures forever. He is still putting up with the sinful antics of man. He is still extending mercy.

Sometimes you may wonder why the Lord goes on and on extending mercy when it appears the world is getting worse and worse.

Man's inhumanity to man is on the increase. Man's ability to inflict abuse and punishment upon his fellowman, upon the environment, and upon the animal kingdom seems to be increasing. Yet, God goes on and on showing His mercy.

So we need to show mercy, but mercy is not being sentimental nor is it being a doormat.

The next thing Paul listed is *kindness*. You may say, "Yeah, but I don't feel like being kind." Well, sometimes I don't either. But the Word says to be kind. *Mercy* and *loving-kindness* seem to go together. It is hard to show one without the other.

The next thing is *humbleness of mind* and *meekness*. The first means not being puffed up and prideful, not thinking more of yourself than you ought (Rom. 12:3). The second characteristic is King James English for "teachableness." Meekness (the Greek word *prautes*) does *not* mean weakness.

Vine's Expository Dictionary[13] says:

> It is only the humble heart which is also the meek, and which, as such, does not fight against God and more or less struggle and contend with Him. This meekness, however, being first of all a meekness before God, is also such in the face of men, even evil men....

---

[13]Vine's, Vol. 3, p. 56.

> The meaning of *prautes* is not readily expressed in English, for the terms meekness, mildness, commonly used, suggest weakness... whereas *prautes* does nothing of the kind .... It must be clearly understood, therefore, that the meekness manifested by the Lord and commended to the believer is the fruit of power .... the Lord was "meek" because He had the infinite resources of God at His command.

Another way of describing *meekness* is to say a meek person is not concerned with self at all, not depressed at being mistreated nor lifted up at being noticed. Christians are urged to show "...*all meekness unto all men*" (Titus 3:2).

A misunderstanding about *meekness* has kept a lot of men out of the Kingdom of God. Many men have felt they had to be spineless jellyfishes, a Casper Milquetoast, or allow themselves to be spit on, walked on, pushed around and in general treated anyway anyone else wanted to treat them.

All you have to do is to look at the life of Jesus to see that He was meek; yet, He was never pushed around. He was not weak. A *meek* person is someone who recognizes his potential, his power and his ability but who does not take advantage of that.

Humility does not mean, "I'm so unworthy." That is not humility; that is stupidity! The Bible says we are "a royal priesthood" (1 Pet. 2:9). How can you be a royal priesthood and be unworthy? How can you be "an old sinner saved by grace"? God does not have any sinner-children. All of His children are redeemed.

Humility is in a person who knows that all credit belongs to *"God which worketh in you both to will and to do of his good pleasure"* (Phil. 2:13).

Longsuffering is the last thing mentioned in verse 12. Most people think longsuffering means "suffering a long time," which sounds logical. However, that is not right. Longsuffering is simply having the willingness and strength to put up with one another, with "patience."[14] And we can do that, because we have *Christ in us, the hope of glory* (Col. 1:27).

> **Forbearing one another, and forgiving one another, if any man have a quarrel against any: even as Christ forgave you, so also do ye.**
> **(Col. 3:13)**

Forbearing one another means to put up with,[15] and *longsuffering* means "to put up with for a long time!"

We have to tolerate one another, or we will never make it. None of us is perfect. We are simply "being perfected," being made mature. We need one another. Those in the family of God should especially look out for one another, because we are more brothers and sisters than natural family members are. Blood relationships are temporary, but spiritual relationships are eternal.

I thank God that I do not have anything against anyone. I would not waste time holding a grudge against someone. We *have* to forgive. Think of all the

---

[14]Strong's, *#3115.*
[15]Ibid., *#430.*

times when God has forgiven us. I pray for people who say unkind things about me. That does not mean it was right for someone to gossip or talk about me or about you. However, two wrongs do not make a right.

The "bottom line" is not to hold a grudge against anyone and not to insult anyone in return. *"Even as Christ forgave you, so also do ye"* (Col. 3:13).

The Bond of Perfectness

In verse 14, Paul told the Colossians — and through them, he told us — the most important thing to put on is: *love.*

> **And above all these things put on charity** [love],
> **which is the bond of perfectness.**

Above all these means to put love even before mercy, kindness, humbleness, meekness, longsuffering, forgiveness, tolerance and lack of retaliation. The reason is that if you are walking in love, you will not have a problem with the other things.

To "put on love" may sound strange. Where can you get love to put on? The love is in *you*, in your spirit. The love of God has been shed abroad in our hearts by the Holy Spirit (Rom. 5:5). When you were born again, you received all the love you will ever need.

The *love* that was shed abroad in our hearts is *agape*, the God-kind of love, the love Paul describes in First Corinthians 13.[16] What you must do to "put

---

[16]Vine's, Vol. 3, pp. 20,21.

love on'' is to love God with your whole heart, then allow *His* love to filter out of your spirit through your soul and body into actions, deeds, behavior and attitudes that show what is within you.

Love is much like faith: Without works it is dead (James 2:26). Love by itself is nothing, or not real, without a life-style that is consistent with love.

When Paul wrote to "put on love," again he let Christians know that walking in love, acting in love and talking in love is *our* responsibility. When Jesus said all men would know His disciples by the way they loved one another (John 13:35), He meant "by the way we treat one another." Love is no good unless it is demonstrated — unless it is shared.

Under the New Covenant, we do not have the Ten Commandments, because we have a "higher" commandment. Instead of "thou shalt not steal," we have "thou shalt love." Instead of "thou shalt not commit adultery," we have "thou shalt love," and so forth. If you love God and your neighbor as yourself (Matt. 19:19), you are not going to steal or do any of the other negative things that say you are not walking in love.

Do you realize, however, that stealing means more than taking someone's money, car or possessions? Stealing can mean taking away someone's character, his or her good name and reputation, by lying, gossiping or "bad-mouthing" that person. Repeating something you heard about someone without knowing all the facts or having the facts straight could destroy that person's life.

Many of us do not understand what love is. If we did, we would not harm one another in the ways we do.

Walking in love, Paul wrote, is the bond of perfectness. That means love is the *mark of maturity*. You can tell a mature Christian by the way he treats his brothers and sisters, the way he acts toward his family and friends and the way he respects the authorities set over him. Without the love of God, no one can act like Jesus in all of these areas.

So begin to "put on love" in order to have the sign of maturity showing in your life.

The Peace of God Must Reign

Love, the mark of maturity, will bring peace in your heart and unity in the Body of Christ, Paul wrote.

> **And let the peace of God rule in your hearts, to the which also ye are called in one body; and be ye thankful.**
>
> **(Col. 3:15)**

Paul did not tell church members at Colossae to "go somewhere and get the peace of God." He did not even tell them to come to church and get it. What this verse means is that you *already* have the peace of God in your hearts.

God put it there as part of the new creature He made you into at your conversion. *Your* part is to let peace rule.

Jesus explained this principle in the sixteenth chapter of John's Gospel:

> **These things have I spoken unto you, that in me ye might have peace. In the world ye shall have tribulation: But be of good cheer; I have overcome the world.**
>
> **(John 16:33)**

> **Peace I leave with you, my peace I give unto you: not as the world giveth, give I unto you. Let not your heart be troubled, neither let it be afraid.**
>
> **(John 14:27)**

Notice the close correspondence between what Jesus said and what Paul wrote. Jesus left us His peace, the peace from above (James 3:17), not the kind of peace the world talks about. Then Jesus said, *"Let not..."*; in other words, *you* have authority over your heart. Do not let trouble or fear come into your heart.

If anxiety, worry or fear attack you, it is your fault if you receive them. They certainly were not given to you by Jesus. They are part of the old man, not the new one.

I have shocked some people who asked me to pray for them to have the peace of God, when I said, "No, I won't pray for you to have the peace of God. *You already have it.*"

And, of course, their problem is that they are going by their feelings instead of faith. You may be thinking, "But I don't feel peaceful. How do I get peace to work for me?"

All you have to do is to ask yourself, "How does a peaceful person act? How does a peaceful person think?" Then you begin to act and think that way, and the peace of God that already is within you will rise up and have authority in your life. You can be at peace in the middle of the storm.

In Mark 4:35-40, we are told how Jesus was at peace in the middle of the storm while the disciples were confessing that they were about to perish. But Jesus got up from His nap when they panicked, and He rebuked the waves and the wind.

He said, "Peace, be still!" to the storm (Mark 4:39) because He had the peace of God within Him.

God's peace is not based on our circumstances. You can always tell whether a Christian is walking by faith or by sight. If they are upset and anxious by what is going on around them, they are walking according to the circumstances.

At one time, I thought I was a "victim of circumstances." I thought if my circumstances could be changed to be more in line with my desires, I would have inner peace, satisfaction and tranquility. But when I saw from the Word that my circumstances have nothing to do with whether my heart is troubled or at peace, I began to be at peace.

Why did God make Jesus the Head of the Church and His recreated brothers and sisters the Body of Christ? Why do the Scriptures always show us in relationship to Jesus as a total unit? That is because wherever Jesus is, we are, and wherever we are, He is. In other words, God is not "calling" us the Body. He is stating facts. We *are* the Body and Jesus is the Head.

God does not see Fred Price when He looks at me; He sees Jesus. And He expects us to grow into enough maturity to act like Jesus. In the midst of the hardships of His ministry, the persecution, misunderstandings and outright hatred, Jesus walked in peace. He had the peace of God within Him through all of the events surrounding His trial and crucifixion.

When Paul wrote, ''. . . *let the peace of God rule,''* he meant for the Colossians to let peace control their lives. Some Christians today are frustrated and upset. Usually it is because they do not have the peace of God ruling in their lives. And the peace is not ruling because they are walking contrary to the Word of God.

His peace will not work in the midst of disobedience. You may not be stealing, lying or commiting adultery. But if you are worrying, you are sinning. You are in disobedience to the Word, if you worry or fret over circumstances that come against you in life.

The last thing Paul wrote in verse 15 was for them to *be thankful*. I am thankful for the peace of God in my life and in my church.

10

Do Everything as Unto the Lord (Col. 3:16-15 and Col. 4:1-18)

The entire book of Colossians (as well as Paul's other epistles) is a guideline for Christian living. However, in the final verses of chapters three and four, Paul particularly covers a lot of territory concerning the victorious Christian life-style.

He told the Colossians briefly but concisely about worship services. He wrote about relationships between husbands and wives, parents and children and bosses and servants (or as we say today, "employees"). And he wrote about prayer, right speech and making time count.

> **Let the word of Christ dwell in you richly in all wisdom; teaching and admonishing one another in psalms and hymns and spiritual songs, singing with grace in your hearts to the Lord.**
>
> **(Col. 3:16)**

This verse means that if the Word of Christ is not "dwelling in you richly," it is because you are not letting the Word take authority in your life.

You must understand that *you* are in control. That means you can go as far as you want to go and as fast as you want to go. If God were *making* all this work, we would all be at the same level of spiritual maturity — and we would all be maturing at the same time.

Have you wondered why some people seem to be more spiritually advanced than others? That is because they are controlling their advancement. They are hungry for God and for His Word, and the hungrier they are, the more they feed on it. What you get out of anything is in direct proportion to what you put into it. This is true of spiritual things as well as worldly.

For example, if you take fifteen to sixteen units for academic credit every semester, it will not take you long to get a college degree. By the same token, if you take only three or four units, it will take you five to six times as long to get a degree. You may finally get there, but it is going to take you much longer.

In addition to teaching and helping one another with hymns and spiritual songs, Paul said we should be... "singing with grace in your hearts to the Lord." He is talking about singing in the spirit.

Many songs today are not the type of songs the Bible talks about. These songs will not help you, because they are too full of unbelief. They are not consistent with the Word, and they do not give you what you need to know in order to operate in wisdom.

You can hear things subconsciously without purposely listening to them. Perhaps you have the radio on a music station as you drive home from work, and you are concentrating on traffic and thinking about other things. You do not consciously listen to a song and decide to memorize it. Yet, after you get home, you may find yourself whistling that melody.

That is why you need to be careful about what you hear, so that when you sing a song, it will be one that inspires you, encourages you and lifts you up. You should make sure the words are consistent with the Word of God. Some songs are beautiful, musically speaking; yet, they do not contain the Word of God. Listening to them will not bring out the peace of God in you.

The word *dwell* means to ''live in and take up residence in.'' Literally, verse sixteen means to let the Word of Christ live inside of you. Again, the word *let* implies that you have the responsibility to do this.

> **And whatsoever ye do in word or deed, do all in the name of the Lord Jesus, giving thanks to God and the Father by him.**
>
> **(Col. 3:17)**

''Whatsoever'' means the same thing as ''all.'' Paul wrote that whatever we do, whether it is speaking or doing things, we are to do them in the name of Jesus.

How could you commit adultery in the name of Jesus? How could you lie in the name of Jesus? How could you bear false witness in the name of Jesus? How could you marry someone who is not a Christian and be ''unequally yoked'' in the name of Jesus?

This verse probably answers ninety-nine percent of all the questions Christians ask concerning what is lawful for Christians to do. The Bible is not a book on a lot of ''do's and don'ts.'' But there are many basic principles that can be applied in just about every situation. Anything you want to do that you cannot do "as unto the Lord," obviously is something you should not do.

This Scripture answers such questions as, "Can I, in Jesus' name, as a Christian, smoke pot, or get drunk, or shoot up with heroin, or get involved in an illicit sexual situation?" Can you do those things in the name of Jesus? If you cannot, then you should not be doing them!

Guidelines for Relationships

Wives, submit yourselves unto your own husbands, as it is fit in the Lord. Husbands, love your wives, and be not bitter against them. Children, obey your parents in all things: for this is well pleasing unto the Lord. Fathers, provoke not your children to anger, lest they be discouraged. Servants, obey in all things your masters according to the flesh; not with eyeservice, as menpleasers; but in singleness of heart, fearing God: And whatsoever ye do, do it heartily, as to the Lord, and not unto men; Knowing that of the Lord ye shall receive the reward of the inheritance: for ye serve the Lord Christ. But he that doeth wrong shall receive for the wrong which he hath done: and there is not respect of persons. (Col. 3:18-25)

Verse 18 sounds a little strange, does it not? Whose husband would a wife submit to, if not her own? However, I believe what Paul wanted us to see in this area is how Satan has tricked many people.

As a husband, you have no business having female friends other than jointly with your wife. As a wife, you should have no male friends other than jointly with your husband. If you cannot talk to your wife or husband, then you have never taken the time to develop a communicating, caring relationship.

Your spouse should be a mate, a helper, a lover and a *friend*. Wives ought to be all in all to their husbands, and husbands should be the same to their wives. It is dangerous for a husband or wife to develop an intimacy, which can come from working closely together, with a member of the opposite sex. Such intimacy is unlawful and, therefore, it is to be avoided at all costs.

"Be not bitter against them." This is another odd thing to say. Yet, there are many occasions and areas where bitterness can arise in a marriage.

If you are a married man, and your wife is not all you want her to be, help her out. For instance, if you don't like the way she wears her hair, get some beauty books or magazines that show different hairstyles and suggest that she try one until you both find one that you like and that enhances or brings out her best physical qualities. You can do the same with makeup, clothes and jewelry.

Do not criticize or judge her. Do not be bitter against her. This is an active requirement for a Christian marriage. Husbands are *required* to love their wives. This verse means a husband should treat his wife as he would want to be treated.

Paul's admonition to children concerns minor children. He is not talking about men and women who are married letting parents run their households. The *husband* is the head of the house, not his parents, nor hers.

Also, I find it interesting that Paul told fathers not to provoke their children. Why did he not mention this to mothers? This is because the father is the head of the household. He is supposed to decide the guidelines and the rules of the home, and the mother is to see they are carried out.

The words *"to anger"* are italicized in the King James Version of the Bible. That means they were not in the original text but have been added.

Paul said not to "ride" your children, and do not try to make them into carbon copies of you, or to fulfill visions and dreams of yours which you never got to accomplish. Let your children find their own course. Do not try to make them become a doctor or a lawyer or a football hero because that was your desire, and you never got a chance to fulfill your dream.

Sometimes parents are "uptight" about their children's scholastic abilities. Some children have to make all A's or face parental disapproval. Some even get punished. What is the big deal about an A? There are many students who were D students in school, but became A students in life. Others were A students in school but are F's in life.

Children, particularly boys, need a father figure in the home. If you are a father, I encourage you to take your rightful place as a father and be the best you can be. It may cost you time and effort, but the effort exerted will be invaluable to your children and worth it to you later in life. It also will have eternal value.

Employer/Employee Relationships

Some people have taken chapter 4, verse 1, which talks about servants and have attempted to legalize slavery or to excuse having slaves. You can make the Bible say anything you want, if you take verses out of the social, political or cultural context of the time, or out of the surrounding verse-context. Few verses in the Bible are to be interpreted solely on their own basis. John 3:16 and most of the Book of Proverbs stand alone, but the majority of verses do not.

In the day when Paul was writing, Christianity was brand-new, and slavery was an ancient institution destined to last another 1,800 years in most of the world. Servants included those hired, those in "bond" for a certain period of time and those owned, which were called slaves.

Servants or slaves were not of any one race or nationality. Even Jewish people in Jesus' day owned slaves. Some were their own countrymen, who had given themselves in bond to pay off debts or because they were too poor to provide for themselves and had no ability to make a living.

Jewish law from the time of Moses had provided for all slaves to be freed every seventh year and released with enough clothes and money to start over. However, by the time of the early church, this was part of Moses' law that usually was not kept.

Rome had made slaves of captives from all the nations they had conquered, as had Greece, Persia, Babylon and Egypt before them. A few years before Christ was born, Rome had conquered the British Isles, and there even were "Brit" slaves to be found in the city of Rome in Paul's day.

Some of these servants, along with their masters, had become born again. Paul wrote instructions in several of his letters to cover these situations. Masters were to be fair and kind, and slaves or servants (employees) were to give a good day's work, obey those in authority over them and do their work as unto the Lord.

Today, we could say it this way: "Employees, obey your employer in all things that do not conflict with the Word of God. Don't obey orders reluctantly or rebelliously after the flesh, or just to win praise. But do the best work you can with a heart that is set on pleasing and reverencing God."

When you work for someone, he is your "master," is he not? He is the one making the rules, paying the wages and setting down guidelines for your job. Paul was saying to work as though you were working directly for the Lord, instead of doing things to please men.

The Lord will see that you are promoted and rewarded. Look on your job as an opportunity to show the very best you can do and as an opportunity to make your life a testimony for God.

When people look at you, will they say, "He is the best worker on staff"? Will they say, "That is the most dependable person we have, the easiest person to get along with, faithful and always on time"?

Or will they say, "Man, that joker is late all the time. He misses one or two days every month from work. You cannot count on him. He half does his job. Did you say he is a Christian? That is what I always say about those Christians: they are lazy good-for-nothings"?

Whatsoever ye do, do it heartily, as to the Lord, and not unto men.

(Col. 3:23)

Paul pointed out that those who do this know that they will receive the reward of the inheritance, for they know WHOM they serve: the Lord Jesus Christ. And those who do wrong, he said, will receive consequences for that as well. He made the point that in these things God is no respecter of persons.

The first verse of chapter four actually belongs with the thoughts expressed in the last verses of chapter three.

Masters, give unto your servants that which is just and equal; knowing that ye also have a Master in heaven.

(Col. 4:1)

Again, where he wrote "masters," read "employers" and where he wrote "servants," read "employees." Christians are expected by the Lord to be good and fair employers and obedient and faithful employees.

At Crenshaw Christian Center, we employ some 200 full-time employees with a payroll and benefits package amounting to more than $6,000,000 annually.

It is our desire to compensate our employees according to prevailing wages in our area.

Unfortunately, most Christian organizations live on the poverty syndrome. They expect people to work for as little as possible. We do not. We do the best we can to keep abreast of what the world pays. I am not going to let the devil pay more than God pays. The devil can never outdo God.

Christians have to pay the same for food, gasoline, clothes and housing as non-Christians. So we ought to make the same money as the world, if not more.

If you are an employer with a business of your own, you ought to pay people what they are worth. If they are not worth a good salary, you have no reason to hire them or to keep them employed. Find someone else who is worth a day's pay.

The Lord is going to give us what is just and equal. How can we dare do anything less for our brothers and sisters?

Continue in Prayer

With verse two, Paul switches gears, so to speak, and begins to wind up his letter to this church, a people he loved in the Lord, but whom he had never seen.

> **Continue in prayer, and watch in the same with thanksgiving; Withal praying also for us, that God would open unto us a door of utterance, to speak the mystery of Christ, for which I am also in bonds: That I may make it manifest, as I ought to speak. Walk in wisdom toward them that are without, redeeming the time. Let your speech be always with grace, seasoned**

with salt, that ye may know how ye ought to answer every man.

(Col. 4:2-6)

Paul's last exhortations include:

- Continue in prayer.
- Be thankful in your prayers.
- Redeem the time.
- Keep your speech courteous, but firm.

In other words, as you pray, do not let your prayer be, "My name is Jimmie; I'll take all you'll gimme."

Do some thanksgiving in your praying, and "Do not forget to pray for me," Paul wrote.

He also said, "Pray that God will continue to open doors for me to speak and preach. Although I am in prison for preaching the Word, I intend to continue explaining the mystery of Christ."

"Redeeming the time" literally means to "take advantage of every opportunity you have to do that which is right because you have no guarantee of any time that is ahead of you."

You can believe God and expect to live a long time, and that is right and proper. But you need to take advantage of each moment that you do have, because all you really can count on is what is happening right now, and you cannot afford to procrastinate.

If you have been called into the ministry, do not say, "I'm going to keep doing what I am doing for about five more years, then I'll go out and preach." Do not wait, *unless* the Holy Spirit is giving you a check in your spirit about moving out right now.

I expect to live many, many years to preach the gospel. I intend to preach either until Jesus returns or until I get tired of preaching — which will not be until I am about 125 years old! And I do not mean 125 years the way most people think someone that age might be. I do not intend to be decrepit, blind or senile. No! I mean to preach as long as I live just as I am doing right now.

However, I understand clearly that *now* is all I can really count on. So I preach and teach like a dying man to dying men, because that is what all mortals are. We begin to die the moment we are born.

I have ministered one Sunday, and before the next Sunday, some people in the congregation have gone into eternity. Did they hear the Word that was taught? Did they receive it?

At least they did not go away saying, "I heard Fred Price, but he didn't really say anything that had to do with life. He talked about social issues, social action and some political issues. But he didn't tell me anything about Jesus."

They were not able to go into eternity saying, "I went to church every Sunday, but I rarely heard anything about God. I didn't hear anything about how to live victoriously in Christ."

God forbid that anyone should stand in the Final Judgment, point a finger at me, and say: "I was in your church. I was in your services, but you never said anything about Jesus. You never told me how to get saved, or how to live right, or how to overcome."

The most precious and important thing you have is time, and you cannot get any more of it. You cannot buy more. All you have is NOW! Redeem the time, and make every moment count.

My wife will tell you that I do not let any time go by. I am always doing something. I have my Bible or a book on the Word with me all the time. If I have to go somewhere and sit and wait, I am reading, praying in tongues or studying the Word.

In Chapter 4, verse 6, Paul writes that the way a Christian speaks should reflect the fact that he is a follower of Jesus. His speech should be courteous, kind, and yet, whenever necessary, it should be firm also. There is never any need to be rude or crude, not if your words are seasoned with the substance of the Word of God.

In the balance of this epistle, Paul deals with personal matters. He told the Colossians that he was sending someone in person to tell them all about his condition and to find out details about them to report back to him in Rome. He sent greetings from others in Rome, particularly from Epaphras, one of their brethren who reportedly founded their church.

Then Paul asked that someone from Colossae take his letter and read it to the Christians in Laodicea, where they also had a letter from him that the Colossian Christians were to read. This letter of Paul's has been lost to the Church.

All my state shall Tychicus declare unto you, who is a beloved brother, and a faithful minister and fellowservant in the Lord: Whom I have sent unto you for the same purpose, that he might know your estate,

and comfort your hearts; With Onesimus, a faithful and beloved brother, who is one of you. They shall make known unto you all things which are done here. Aristarchus my fellowprisoner saluteth you, and Marcus, sister's son to Barnabas, (touching whom ye received commandments: if he come unto you, receive him;) And Jesus, which is called Justus, who are of the circumcision. These only are my fellowworkers unto the kingdom of God, which have been a comfort unto me. Epaphras, who is one of you, a servant of Christ, saluteth you, always labouring fervently for you in prayers, that ye may stand perfect and complete in all the will of God. For I bear him record, that he hath a great zeal for you, and them that are in Laodicea, and them in Hierapolis. Luke, the beloved physician, and Demas, greet you. Salute the brethren which are in Laodicea, and Nymphas, and the church which is in his house. And when this epistle is read among you, cause that it be read also in the church of the Laodiceans; and that ye likewise read the epistle from Laodicea.   And say to Archippus, Take heed to the ministry which thou hast received in the Lord, that thou fulfil it. The salutation by the hand of me Paul. Remember my bonds. Grace be with you. Amen.

(Col. 4:7-18)

The Book of Colossians tells us *who we are in Christ:*

• We are heirs and joint-heirs with Christ.

• We have been translated out of the kingdom of darkness into the Kingdom of God's dear Son.

• We are given insight into how to live as Christians and the kinds of things we are to do.

• We are responsible for doing what has been outlined in this practical letter concerning Christian living.

• The Father God will hold us accountable for what we have learned, because He not only has given us His Word, His dear Son, but Himself to reside within us.

We do not have to claim ignorance of spiritual matters. In fact, we cannot claim ignorance. No Christian can claim that he does not know what to do. It is all in the Word.

If you will take what we have studied together in this book and apply it to your life, you will be victorious throughout the rest of your time here on earth.

For a complete list of tapes and books by Fred Price, or to receive his publication, *Ever Increasing Faith Messenger*, write:

Fred Price
Crenshaw Christian Center
P. O. Box 90000
Los Angeles, CA 90009

Books by Frederick K.C. Price, Ph.D.

HIGH FINANCE
(God's Financial Plan: Tithes and Offerings)

HOW FAITH WORKS
(In English and Spanish)

IS HEALING FOR ALL?

HOW TO OBTAIN STRONG FAITH
(Six Principles)

NOW FAITH IS

THE HOLY SPIRIT —
The Missing Ingredient

FAITH, FOOLISHNESS, OR PRESUMPTION?

THANK GOD FOR EVERYTHING?

HOW TO BELIEVE GOD FOR A MATE

MARRIAGE AND THE FAMILY

LIVING IN THE REALM OF THE SPIRIT

THE ORIGIN OF SATAN

CONCERNING THEM WHICH ARE ASLEEP

HOMOSEXUALITY:
State of Birth or State of Mind?

PROSPERITY ON GOD'S TERMS

WALKING IN GOD'S WORD
(Through His Promises)

KEYS TO SUCCESSFUL MINISTRY

NAME IT AND CLAIM IT!
The Power of Positive Confession

THE VICTORIOUS, OVERCOMING LIFE
(A Verse-by-Verse Study of the Book of Colossians)

A NEW LAW FOR A NEW PEOPLE

THE FAITHFULNESS OF GOD

THE PROMISED LAND
(A New Era for the Body of Christ)

Available from your local bookstore